T0358205

Demystifying Business Celebrity

Business celebrities such as Bill Gates, Richard Branson, and Rupert Murdoch are among the most widely recognized, admired, and sometimes even vilified individuals in the world. Like their celebrity peers from the entertainment, sports, arts, and political worlds, business celebrities exert an influence that is pervasive, but difficult to assess, evaluate, and explain.

Business celebrities have been around for as long as big business itself, but this is the first book to provide a systematic exploration of how they are constructed and why they exist. Business celebrities include entrepreneurs, CEOs, and management gurus. The book argues that these individuals are not self-made, but rather are created by a process of widespread media exposure to the point that their actions, personalities, and even private lives function symbolically to represent significant dynamics and tensions prevalent in the contemporary business environment.

Demystifying Business Celebrity raises questions about the impact and significance of the production of celebrity upon our understanding of, and our ability to promote, the practice of leadership in an enlightened manner. The book will prove a useful addition to the enlightened business student's bookshelf and will be informative reading for all those with an interest in business and management.

Eric Guthey is Associate Professor of Intercultural Communication and Management at the Copenhagen Business School, Denmark.

Timothy Clark is Professor of Organizational Behaviour at Durham Business School, UK. He has authored a number of books including *Management Speak*, with David Greatbatch (Routledge, 2005).

Brad Jackson is the Fletcher Building Education Trust Chair in Leadership at the University of Auckland Business School, New Zealand. His previous books include *Management Gurus and Management Fashions* (Routledge, 2001).

Demystifying Business Celebrity

Eric Guthey, Timothy Clark, and Brad Jackson

Routledge
Taylor & Francis Group

LONDON AND NEW YORK

First published 2009
by Routledge
2 Park Square, Milton Park, Abingdon, Oxon OX14 4RN

Simultaneously published in the USA and Canada
by Routledge
605 Third Avenue, New York, NY 10017

Routledge is an imprint of the Taylor & Francis Group, an Informa business

Typeset in Perpetua
by Keystroke, 28 High Street, Tettenhall, Wolverhampton

British Library Cataloguing in Publication Data
A catalogue record for this book is available from the British Library

Library of Congress Cataloguing in Publication Data
Guthey, Eric.
  Demystifying business celebrity / Eric Guthey, Timothy Clark and
Brad Jackson.
     p. cm.
  Includes bibliographical references and index.
  1. Businesspeople—United States. 2. Celebrities—United States.
  I. Clark, Timothy, 1964– II. Jackson, Brad, 1960- III. Title.
  HB615.G884 2009
  650.086′21—dc22
  2008050971

ISBN13: 978–0–415–32781–7 (hbk)
ISBN13: 978–0–415–32782–4 (pbk)
ISBN13: 978–0–203–39069–6 (ebk)

We would like to dedicate this book to our fathers, who are by no means celebrities, yet are worthy of celebration nonetheless.

Contents

Figures

Acknowledgments

Thanks to all at Routledge most especially Simon Alexander, Terry Clague, Sharon Golan, Francesca Heslop, Russell George, and Emma Joyes, for their guidance and assistance in the production of this book. It was a pleasure working with you.

Special thanks are due to Pam Blakemore and Angela Lehn for their diligence, patience, and continued good humor in preparing the list of references for the book.

Our appreciation also extends to Hwee Khoo who conducted some of the earlier bibliographic research and who introduced us to the Asian "Celebrity CEO."

We also thank Professor Lilie Chouliaraki of the London School of Economics for her behind-the-scenes help in making it possible to secure permissions for the images that appear in this book.

We would also like to acknowledge all of our colleagues at the Copenhagen Business School, Durham Business School, and the University of Auckland Business School for their collegial support, intellectual stimulation, and continued encouragement.

Portions of this book are reproduced by permission of SAGE Publications Ltd., London, Los Angeles, New Delhi, Singapore and Washington DC, from Timothy A.R. Clark, 'The fashion of management fashion: a surge too far?', *Organization*, copyright (© Sage Publications, 2004).

Portions of this book are reproduced by permission of SAGE Publications, Los Angeles, London, New Delhi, Singapore and Washington DC, from Timothy Clark and David Greatbatch, 'Management fashion as image-spectacle: the production of management best-sellers', *Management Communication Quarterly* , copyright (© Sage Publications, 2003).

Portions of Chapter 4 are drawn from Guthey E. and Jackson B. (2005) "CEO Portraits and the Authenticity Paradox," *Journal of Management Studies*, vol. 42, no. 5: 1057–82.

Finally, not for the first or the last time, we would like to offer our heartfelt thanks to the real "celebrities" of our lives: our wives, Fran, Penny, and Jacquie, and the "stars of the future," our progeny Maddie, Johannes, and Thea; Max and India; and Devan and Colin. We look forward to a time when we can all come together to properly "celebrate" the completion of another book!

1 Why demystifying business celebrities matters

Britney Spears. O.J. Simpson. Whitney Houston. Michael Jackson. Boy George. Mike Tyson. We know their faces. We know intimate details about their private lives, often more than we care to know. Aside from their achievements in music, movies, sports, and entertainment, they have all enjoyed a surfeit of media exposure, and the wealth that comes along with it. At one time or another each has dominated the tabloid media spotlight. They share the signature celebrity hallmark of having become famous, at least in part, just for being famous.

These particular celebrities have something else in common. In one way or another each has lost a large part of his or her celebrity veneer and suffered scandal, legal action, or financial mismanagement, losing millions or even going bankrupt. Perhaps we should not make too much of this latter, rather infamous distinction. After all, celebrities do not attract media attention or fan devotion primarily for their skills at managing wealth or running a company.

But what about people who do become famous for such activities—the Jack Welches, and the Rupert Murdochs? Are business celebrities *really* better at managing their businesses than everyone else? Is that the reason they become famous in the first place? And what is the connection between tabloid celebrities of the Spears/Jackson/Tyson variety and celebrated business figures like Welch, Murdoch, Bill Gates, Steve Jobs, Carly Fiorina, Martha Stewart, Donald Trump, Steven Covey, and Tom Peters?

Take a management guru like Peters. *Time* magazine reported in the spring of 2007 that members of the consulting firm formerly known as the Tom Peters Company felt that things actually *improved* for them after the world-renowned author and inspirational speaker had left the company. "The partners of the renamed Bluepoint Leadership Development say that they are better managed without the world-famous management consultant and author," the magazine pointed out, citing "higher revenues, doubled profitability, loyalty from old clients and a roster of new ones like Starbucks, DHL and GE." Remarked one of the company's partners, "Fortune called Tom Peters the Ur-guru of management, but apparently not when it comes to running his own company" (Russo 2007).

In his defense, Peters explained that he had "worked at building a brand, but not through training and consulting," because he was "an ideas person." He clearly has a point if you believe that the primary function of a management guru is not to run companies, but to inspire others to do so by means of blockbuster speaking engagements and best-selling books. From this perspective it makes perfect sense, as *Time* concluded, that Tom Peters "was never interested in running anything but Tom Peters." In general, it seems that management gurus are excused for promoting themselves shamelessly. Perhaps no one really expects them to do anything else.

Unlike Peters, Sir Richard Branson *is* famous for running his own businesses well. His mail-order record company, which he started out of the back of his car when he was 20 years old, has grown into a vast, diversified empire that includes airlines, trains, travel services, media and communications, music, leisure and entertainment, branded consumer goods, health care, personal finance, even wine, bridal services, alternative energies, and space tourism. Still, the identity of the Virgin empire remains so wrapped up in Branson himself that, like Tom Peters, he appears constantly occupied with managing his own personal brand as well. Indeed, Branson and Virgin are inseparable, so that both the company and the media invariably spice up news about Virgin with tales of Branson's flamboyant personality and thrill-seeking exploits. "Whether he's ballooning across oceans or in a dogfight with British Airways, Richard Branson lives, works and plays on the edge," declared a typical media profile in *Sports Illustrated* in 1999.

Of course, Branson himself has done a great deal to create and maintain such impressions, setting aside a full 25 percent of his time for public relations activities. The aforementioned *Sports Illustrated* profile allegedly came about because Branson made his private Caribbean island available as a backdrop for the magazine's 1999 swimsuit issue, in which the profile itself appeared. In a similar arrangement, director Martin Campbell gave Branson and his son a cameo appearance in his recent James Bond film, *Casino Royale*, in exchange for the use of a Virgin jet. As *Time* magazine recently observed in an article on the launch of Branson's venture into space tourism, which also took place on Necker Island, "the hyper-entrepreneurial Branson . . . has an unlimited appetite for outlandish promotional stunts" (Thomas 2007).

Figure 1.1 "Richard Branson . . . on Necker Island . . . in a Spacesuit."

Source: Reproduced with the generous permission of photographer Brian Smith (http//: www.briansmithphoto.com)

   The case of Richard Branson also makes clear that it takes more than one self-promoting hyper-entrepreneur to pull off such media stunts. It takes a well-oiled publicity machine, in fact a network of interlocking publicity and media engines running in tandem. The iconic and decidedly promotional photo that accompanied the *Time* article about Virgin Galactic was conceived not by Branson's PR flaks, but by *Time*'s deputy photo editor Dietmar Liz-Lepiorz. The photograph was shot by freelance celebrity photographer

Brian Smith, who describes the initial concept as simply "Richard Branson . . . on Necker Island . . . in a spacesuit" (see Figure 1.1). The spacesuit in question did not come from Virgin Galactic's own storeroom or spaceship airlock. It was shipped to Branson's island by *Time's* Los Angeles photo editor Martha Bardach, who rented it from a movie costume rental supplier in Hollywood. As we discuss in later chapters, all of these different types of people—journalists, editors, photographers, publicists, even movie directors —function as what we call business culture intermediaries. They make the celebrity magic happen, and they are central to what we call the manufactured co-production of business celebrities like Branson and Peters. Even the man in charge of Branson's space tourism company himself is a business culture intermediary. Before taking the reins of Virgin Galactic, president Will Whitehorn ran Virgin's public relations and brand development for nearly twenty years.

In this book we explore the significance of business celebrities themselves, as well as the workings of the interlocking networks of business culture intermediaries that co-produce and sustain them. Our motivation for broaching this topic is *not* that celebrity has become such a widespread and all-encompassing phenomenon in the twenty-first century that it has spread *even* into the business world. According to this sort of "that-was-then-this-was-now" argument, business practitioners (and scholars thereof) used to have to worry only about the nuts-and-bolts practicalities of running a business. Now the proliferation of media channels and the encroachment of celebrity culture mean that business leaders have to worry about reputation, about fame, and about the way that celebrity works too. From this perspective the business celebrity is a Johnny-come-lately to the media spotlight who, many argue, should stop prancing about like a *Big Brother* contestant and stick to his or her balance sheets.

We do not share this view of business celebrity as a passing fad or superficial phenomenon that distracts managers away from "real business issues." To the contrary, business celebrities remain a perennial object of media fascination in large part because they function both to highlight and to smooth over some of the key cultural and ideological tensions generated by the dominance of business institutions in contemporary society, as well as some of the key challenges and struggles faced by the people who must work and manage inside these institutions. And these struggles are very real.

We maintain that the connections between business and celebrity point towards something central to both institutions, and not simply because celebrity is a business the point of which is to make lots of money. From a broader, cultural perspective, business celebrity functions as a forum (however compromised by commercial or promotional hype) for concerns and debates about what it means to be an individual in a complex, modern society, and what it means for individuals to work in complex, commercial organizations. In this regard our argument about business celebrities echoes Richard Dyer's argument about Hollywood stars. "Stars articulate what it is to be a human being in contemporary society," said Dyer. "That is, they express the particular notion we hold of the person." But his use of the term "we" should not be taken to imply that everyone agrees about such issues, because Hollywood stars and business celebrities alike are complex, ambiguous, and open to various interpretations. In Dyer's words "they are not straightforward affirmations of individualism," because they "articulate both the promise and the difficulty that the notion of the individual presents" (Dyer 1986: 8; quoted in Turner 2004: 103). If we read between the lines of the many other functions and purposes it serves, we can see that the celebrity system provides a testing ground, and sometimes a soapbox, for ideas and arguments about how it is possible for an individual to take action, to stand out from the crowd, and to make a difference in the face of vast commercial, corporate, and social forces beyond their control.

These issues have vexed many people, including individual, rank-and-file managers, ever since the advent of large corporate institutions towards the end of the nineteenth century. The rise of big business challenged previously dominant conceptions of the individual and of individual agency. It turned the supposedly level playing field of the marketplace into a mountain range of unequal power relations, with a few individuals occupying the peaks and everyone else toiling down below. One result of this upheaval was to direct an intense amount of public and media attention towards the individuals who dominated the new business landscape, and towards the unprecedented power and wealth they came to enjoy. Muckraking exposés thrust business leaders into the limelight in new ways during this period—such as Ray Stannard Baker's 1901 *Windsor Magazine* profile of J.P. Morgan as "the emperor of trusts," and Ida Tarbell's scathing history of John D. Rockefeller's Standard Oil Company, published in *McClure's Magazine* from 1902 to 1904. Tarbell ended her 19-part series with a scathing character study of the "money-mad" Rockefeller, concluding that "our national life is on every side distinctly poorer, uglier, meaner, for the kind of influence he exercises." Visual images of business leaders during the muckraking era often portrayed them as dangerous giants who threatened the sovereignty of democratically elected governments (see Figures 1.2 and 1.3).

Figure 1.2 "Jack and the Wall Street Giants," from *Puck* magazine, January 1904. Artist: Joseph Keppler (1904).

Source: This image is in the public domain. Library of Congress (http://www.loc.gov)

JACK AND THE WALL STREET GIANTS

Such negative media portrayals of the business leaders who came to be known as the "Robber Barons" did not go unchallenged. With considerable encouragement from big business itself, the media also began to produce counter-narratives and images that cast business leaders as figures to be revered and emulated, paragons of virtue, heroic, self-made entrepreneurs, patrons of the arts, and humanitarian philanthropists (see the austere portrait of Rockefeller by John Singer Sargent, Figure 1.4). Roland Marchand has argued convincingly that the entire field of commercial public relations arose during this period from the need to allay widespread fears that corporations were menacing forces, powerful new creatures without a soul that would destroy the fabled fabric of small-town America (Marchand 1998). In their efforts to change this impression, Marchand makes clear, the new public

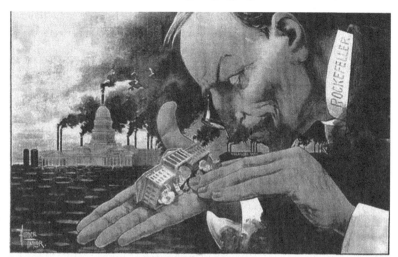

Figure 1.3 "The Trust Giant's Point of View. 'What a funny little government.'" A caricature of John D. Rockefeller from *Verdict* magazine, January 22, 1900. Artist: Horace Taylor (Taylor 1900).

Source: This image is in the public domain. EHistory archive at Ohio State University (http://ehistory.osu.edu/osu/mmh/USCartoons/Verdict/HT/22Jan1900.cfm)

Figure 1.4 Portrait of John D. Rockefeller by John Singer Sargent, *c.* 1917.

Source: This image is in the public domain. Wikimedia Commons (http://commons.wikimedia.org)

relations professionals quickly seized upon corporate leaders as the human faces that would personify corporate benevolence. The tension between these two opposing visions of business leadership—Robber Baron or philanthropist, greedy imperialist or benevolent humanitarian—has never been resolved, and they still dominate the portrayal of business celebrities in the media.

If the need to personify and humanize the power of big business gave rise to public relations, and if the rise of public relations in turn contributed to the predominance of the modern celebrity, then business figures are more crucial for understanding the phenomenon of celebrity than previously imagined. As we touch upon in the next chapter, scholars of celebrity, most of them in the fields of cultural studies and media theory, largely ignore business icons. Many of these scholars maintain that early film stars provided the model for modern celebrity. But even before Hollywood celebrities like Douglas Fairbanks, Mary Pickford, and Charlie Chaplin captured the public imagination, figures like John D. Rockefeller, Andrew Carnegie, J.P. Morgan, Thomas Edison, and Henry Ford had become highly visible repositories of the tensions and debates generated by social, commercial, and technological changes that contributed to the development of the Hollywood film industry itself. Business figures are not newcomers to the game of celebrity. In this book we argue that they helped make up the rules of the game in the first

Figure 1.5 An enraged J.P. Morgan striking photographer with cane, *c.* May 11, 1910.

Source: This image is in the public domain. Library of Congress (http://www.loc.gov)

Figure 1.6 An enraged Britney Spears following in Morgan's footsteps, February 21, 2007.

Source: Reproduced with the generous permission of X17 Agency
(http://www.x17agency.com)

place. Thus, when Britney Spears stunned the media consuming public by using an umbrella to lash out at the media for hounding her, she was acting out a role developed almost a century before by American financier J.P. Morgan (see Figures 1.5 and 1.6).

At this point some readers may question our suggestions that celebrity is a uniquely modern phenomenon, or that the rise of business celebrity around the turn of the twentieth century was something particularly new. After all, Alexander the Great was famous. So were Socrates, Julius Caesar, Queen Elizabeth, Shakespeare, Benjamin Franklin, and Napoleon. More than just famous, in fact, all of these figures and countless others we could mention throughout history became *iconic*, in both a figurative and a visual sense. And if we want to define celebrities as icons, then we have to grapple with the religious connotations of that term, perhaps even including on our list the most iconic religious figure in western history. Does it make sense to consider Jesus Christ a celebrity, too?

There is certainly merit in placing the phenomenon of celebrity in just this kind of broad, historical perspective, as Leo Braudy does in his mammoth book, *The Frenzy of Renown: Fame and Its History*. Drawing on a wealth of historical detail, Braudy makes clear that "our involvement with the famous . . . is hardly an invention of the twentieth century" (1997: 10). As he explains, "in every era and culture of the West since the classical age, fame has been a complex word into which is loaded much that is deeply believed about the nature of the individual, the social world, and whatever exists beyond both" (1997: 586). But Braudy also argues that the history of fame is a history of the *changing* ways that people have understood that word, and the changing contexts in which they have done so. From this perspective, the decline in divinely ordained monarchical authority symbolized by the French and American revolutions, the rise of the bourgeois merchant class, and the industrialization of human labor and productive technologies all contributed to the transformation of the nature of fame itself. During the eighteenth century, "a new-minted industrial age set the scene for individuals to make their way relatively unhampered by the traditions and restrictions of the past," Braudy maintains. And these new freedoms left in their wake a cultural void that had to be filled by something else. He explains further:

> Fame and success therefore became much more important than they had been in a time when the orders of society and the realms of the spirit were more fixed . . . In the past, said Samuel Johnson in the eighteenth century, "man was of a piece." But the new age brought anxieties that only success could allay, when the struggling individual would be gathered into the realm of security and justification that he thought awaited him at the top of the ladder.
>
> (Braudy 1997: 7)

In what Braudy calls an increasingly "more crowded, corporate, and collective world," distinguishing oneself became more important to more people (1997: 8). At the same time, the means and technologies available for achieving such distinction were changing rapidly. With the development of linotype machines and massive, high-volume printing presses in the nineteenth century came the rise of the great newspapers—the *New York Herald*, the *New York Times*, the *Chicago Tribune* in the United States, and the *Daily Herald* in England. Fierce competition between these newspapers soon led to the spread of exactly the kind of sensationalist journalism that both promotes and thrives on a public thirst for elevating celebrities and then tearing them back down. Equally significant for the transformation of fame during this period was the advent of photography, and its increasing availability to the masses. Even the invention of the daguerreotype, all in all a rather cumbersome device for creating images, created a vigorous market for portraits, thereby reinforcing the cultural urge to elevate the importance of the individual. The subsequent development of more efficient means of reproducing images, eventually even moving images, completed the transformation of the human face and personality into commodities for mass distribution and consumption.

All of these developments occurred in the context of the rise of corporate capitalism, the innovation of mass production technologies, the spread of mass market advertising, and the substantial reordering of western cultural priorities around consumption and consumer desire. One effect of these sweeping changes was to give rise to a new type of fame, and we find it helpful to distinguish it from what came earlier with the term "celebrity." Fame in the broader sense refers to public acclaim and widespread recognition. Celebrity is something more specific. As we discuss in more detail in the next chapter, Christopher Rojek defines fame or renown as "the informal attribution of distinction on an individual within a given social network." Rojek insists that celebrity occurs only when fame becomes a commodity produced and consumed via the commercial media in a manner that generates a particular form of abstract consumer desire (2001: 12, 187ff.). From this perspective, even if Alexander the Great was the first famous person in human history, as Braudy points out, he was not a celebrity, because he never became a cultural commodity subject to the industrial, mass-mediated process of *celebrification*. While fame has existed for centuries, celebrity did not appear until fame became big business.

From this perspective, celebrity does not simply happen naturally, even to deserving individuals. In fact, talking about celebrities as if they were individuals glosses over some of the most central and powerful aspects of the phenomenon. The production of celebrity as a cultural commodity takes place by means of a very distinctive industrial process which we describe in detail in the next chapter. This process depends on the efforts of a variety of loosely connected cultural intermediaries—among them the photographers, paparazzi, journalists, editors, publicists, agents, and public relations professionals we mentioned earlier. All of these players have their own interests and agendas, but the net effect of their often scattered efforts is the orchestrated co-production, cross-promotion, and circulation of a rather strange species of mediated persons. To the extent that we can talk about celebrities as individuals at all, then, they are commodified individuals widely attributed with unique and noteworthy characteristics and actions, images of whom are produced, distributed, consumed, and recycled via commercial and popular channels in ways that encourage relatively large numbers of people to cultivate strong mediated relationships with them.

The process by means of which celebrities get constructed and distributed exerts a strong influence over the shape of the final product. Several factors —the multiple inputs and interests involved, the cross-fertilization across markets and media platforms, and the hybrid nature of celebrities themselves as both persons and commodities—together have the effect of both high-lighting and blurring the boundaries between several spheres of experience conventionally understood as being separate and distinct. These include the boundaries between what is public and private, commercial and non-commercial, individual and social, cultural and psychological, staged and authentic. The overarching distinction that gets both highlighted and erased by the mediation of celebrity is that between individual agency on the one hand and collective or social agency on the other. Celebrities depend for their status as such on the activities of a complex network of individuals, organizations, commercial forces, and cultural dynamics, but in the process of celebrification and mediation these various activities are folded into or overshadowed by the personalities and actions of the celebrities themselves. As a result celebrities come to represent the possibility and desirability of untrammeled individual agency, power, and distinction in a complex world.

Business celebrities exemplify these many dynamics, and accentuate in particular this latter paradox. They are produced by a crowded industrial process which insists that industry is really just a matter of a few great individuals. They are held up above the rest of the business community by an elaborately constructed scaffolding in such a way that promotes the notion that they can remain floating in mid-air by virtue of their own innate skills and exemplary characteristics. For the purposes of this book we therefore define business celebrity as *the production of exemplary individuals—entrepreneurs, top executives, management consultant gurus, and others—who are given sustained and widespread exposure in the media to the point where their actions, personalities, and/or private lives function symbolically to represent significant dynamics, and sometimes alleviate significant tensions, prevalent in the contemporary business environment.* Again, these dynamics and tensions revolve in one way or another around the possibility of effective individual agency and the concern that individuals still matter and can make a difference in an ever more complex and globalized business environment.

There are many different types of business celebrity. They serve distinct commercial and cultural functions and articulate different forms of agency and activity, although the different categories overlap and reinforce each other. *Celebrity entrepreneurs*, for example, provide the conceptual or rhetorical foundation for business celebrity by functioning as prototypical figures of pure agency, as creative individuals who have the power to bring products and possibilities into being through the force of their personality, genius, and will. In an article declaring Apple founder Steve Jobs the most powerful business figure of 2007, *Fortune* cited "his ability, time and again, to conjure digital objects of desire from esoteric blends of chips, disks, plastic, and software, and then promote them with his own alluring brand of performance art." The magazine pointed out that "at this moment, no one has more influence over a broader swath of business than Jobs," and that he had always exerted his distinctive brand of influence and power "with the facility of a jujitsu master" (Schlender *et al.* 2007).

Such lone hero entrepreneurs are often portrayed as the scourge or antithesis of large bureaucratic organizations—journalist Michael Lewis has described Netscape founder Jim Clark as a "Disorganization Man" who hates corporate capitalism for the way it encroaches on his freedom (Lewis 2000: 101, Guthey 2004). But narratives about the figures in the grey flannel suits who lead those stuffy organizations often borrow extensively from the adventure-story ethos of the entrepreneur. In this manner *celebrity business leaders and CEOs* can function symbolically to put a human face on the vast networks of power and agency we call corporations by representing their organizations in human and often very personal terms. When corporate leaders become famous enough to peddle advice to the multitudes (see Figure 1.6), they become a hybrid form of management leader and guru combined. *Celebrity management gurus* also function symbolically, rhetorically, and even therapeutically to manage concerns about the prospects for individual agency in a corporate society, but from yet another angle. Often with the fervor of an evangelical preacher, management gurus shore up faith in the idea that like business celebrities themselves, everyday employees and rank-and-file middle-management types can act decisively and make a difference in an increasingly complex and confusing world.

This book does not attempt to catalogue all of these different types of business celebrity, nor even to list and describe the most famous business celebrities in the world. We focus primarily on celebrity CEOs and management gurus, but not because we consider them more significant than entrepreneurs, financiers, Wall Street traders, marketing and sales people, Hollywood agents, or other business figures. Our aim is to use these two types of figures to define more clearly what business celebrity is, why it exists, and how it is constructed. Along the way we will have occasion to mention many individual business celebrities, but this is not a book about what makes Donald Trump tick or what Carly Fiorina is really like. We are interested instead in the industrial, promotional, representational, and cultural dynamics that constantly insist that we *should* care about these figures on such a personal level.

Towards this end, the next chapter clarifies and elaborates on our definition of business celebrity by reviewing previous research on the subject. We supplement the rather narrow literature on celebrity in management and organization studies with a wealth of perspectives from sociology and cultural studies, and we develop an approach that emphasizes the connections between the way that business celebrities get produced and the manner in which they embody debates and conflicts over what it means to be a person in a corporate society. We propose a model for understanding business celebrities that emphasizes the crowded nature of the process of celebrification and the central roles played by the many different business culture intermediaries who populate the celebrity industries.

We provide a vivid example of these dynamics in Chapter 3, where we concentrate on the industry that produces management gurus. This chapter begins by highlighting the importance of speaking events and performances to the celebrity status of figures like Tom Peters, Gary Hamel, and Stephen Covey. We also interview publishing industry players and other experts to understand the manner in which blockbuster management advice books are produced. While the nature of their live performances would lead us to characterize these gurus as something more akin to shamans, we conclude, the elaborate network of business culture intermediaries necessary to produce business best-sellers makes clear that such guru figures are best understood as management fashion celebrities.

In Chapter 4 we turn our gaze—literally—to another type of business celebrity, taking a close look at portraits, photographs, and other visual images of celebrity CEOs. As we argue, the centrality of visual representation to the celebrity system requires the cultivation of a form of "visual literacy" in order to "read" the now omnipresent iconography of business celebrity. A closer look at business celebrities from such a perspective helps bring into focus the construction of multiple, often conflicting images of the same business celebrity (Bill Gates, for example), the manner in which even individual images invite multiple perspectives and conflicting interpretations, and the involvement of multiple actors and interests in relational processes of image production, dissemination, and interpretation. Conflicts over how we should interpret such images of business celebrity come to the fore in Chapter 5. Here we consider the tenuous nature of individual claims to business celebrity by examining the recurrent phenomenon of what we have called the CEO celebrity backlash. Anti-celebrity sentiments against business figures like Bill Gates, Enron's Jeffrey Skilling, or Tyco's Dennis Kozlowski are often framed as a critique of the very idea of mixing business and celebrity together in the first place. By contrast, we argue, antipathy towards celebrity figures actually functions as a crucial component of the process of celebrification, and ultimately contributes to the phenomenon of business celebrity over the long term.

Having explored these various industrial, narrative, visual, and performative dynamics of business celebrity, we turn in Chapter 6 to a discussion of the connections between business celebrity and leadership. As we discuss, in recent years the field of leadership studies has produced its own version of the business celebrity backlash. Many leadership scholars are becoming more and more adamant in their criticism of the usefulness of celebrity business leaders, and in their rejection of the kinds of heroic models of leadership implied by the very phenomenon of business celebrity itself. From the celebrity perspective developed in this book, however, these arguments appear misplaced for two important reasons. First of all, a blanket rejection of the idea of celebrity business leadership on the grounds that leadership is (or should be) a much more distributed and social process fails to appreciate the extent to which, as we argue throughout this book, the production and consumption of business celebrities are in fact fundamentally social phenomena involving the input and interaction of a variety of different concerned parties. Second, post-heroic critiques of celebrity business leadership do not fully recognize how the end-products of the process of celebrification bear the marks of all this social interaction. The fact that many celebrity business heroes themselves argue for more distributed and post-heroic styles of management points towards the manner in which business celebrities do not so much argue for heroic forms of leadership as much as they embody concerns and debates about what leadership should be like, and about how business institutions should be run.

In our concluding chapter, we take issue with the manner in which celebrity often is described as the polar opposite of "real" leadership. In fact, we argue, celebrity is a lot like leadership, and the explanatory framework we develop in this book can provide a model for a new approach to the study of leadership itself. Drawing on our discussion of the production of business celebrity, we describe a new approach to studying the production of leadership and the leadership industries. From our production of leadership perspective, it is important to understand leadership as a product of the many organizational, promotional, and discursive practices that characterize the leadership industries. Building on the approach to business celebrity developed in this book, we explore how the creation and promotion of leadership products and services via the leadership industries influence the manner in which leadership itself is practiced and understood.

As this introductory chapter has already made clear, we do not intend to lionize business celebrities uncritically, or to hold up individual business celebrity figures as paragons of business virtue or acumen. But we do hope that this book will clarify some of the lessons to be learned from negative critiques of business celebrity, from positive appreciations of the manner in which celebrity business figures can motivate and inspire others, and from a more thorough investigation of the industrial and cultural dynamics that continue to produce business celebrities, and that show no signs of slowing up in the near future.

2 Business celebrities and the celebrity business

In this chapter we develop our definition of business celebrity as both an interactive, industrial process of cultural production and as the end result of that process. We do so by drawing on previous scholarship on celebrity and tailoring it to the topic at hand. For all their media exposure, business celebrities have received little serious academic scrutiny. This is ironic since, as we explain in this chapter, the growing body of research on celebrity in sociology, cultural, and media studies emphasizes that celebrity is big business, and that celebrities need to be understood as products of the overlapping networks of organizational and economic dynamics that characterize what have been labeled "the celebrity industries" (Turner *et al*. 2000; Turner 2004). Yet few of the scholars doing this work have ventured to make any connections between the celebrity business and business celebrities. The many theories and definitions that emphasize the industrial dynamics of celebrity barely acknowledge the existence of business celebrities, let alone place them at the center of the phenomenon itself.

To find any specific research on business celebrities, therefore, we have to look to the very different academic universe of management and organization studies, which traditionally have shown little interest in popular culture and media studies. In the last few years, however, a handful of researchers have begun to investigate the phenomenon of CEO celebrity, and by extension, celebrity firms. In *Searching for a Corporate Savior* (2002), for example, Khurana delivers a wholesale critique of the executive search industry. His argument leans heavily on a cultural analysis of the shift from managerial to investor capitalism and the space this shift created for the rise of the charismatic CEO. Khurana does not define celebrity or analyze its workings directly, but he makes some very important points about the relationship between celebrity status and shifting understandings of corporate leadership.

Another group of scholars has constructed a model of CEO celebrity that draws on an analysis of the nature of celebrity per se (Hayward *et al*. 2004; Wade *et al*. 2006; Rindova *et al*. 2006). Building on the definition of celebrities by Rein, Kottler, and Stoller as individuals whose names have "attention-getting, interest-riveting and profit-generating value" (1987: 15), these authors define celebrities as social actors who attract high levels of public attention and elicit positive emotional responses from the public, fulfilling audience needs for "gossip, fantasy, identification, status, affiliation, and attachment" (Rindova *et al*. 2006: 51). As we explain below, this research draws its inspiration and strength from previous work on the romance of leadership and the social construction of prominent business leaders (Meindl *et al*. 1985; Chen and Meindl 1991). From this vantage point it directly addresses the issues of agency and individual action we locate at the heart of the business celebrity phenomenon. And this research has performed a valuable service by legitimizing the study of business celebrities in the eyes of an academic audience not generally inclined to take such topics into consideration.

But there is another irony here, because the organizational scholars who recently have begun to explore celebrity have missed what is arguably the central organizational or business angle to the story. Working from within the paradigm of social psychology, they explain CEO celebrity almost exclusively as the creation of journalists who, in the process of trying to explain complex organizational and economic phenomena in simplified form under intense time pressures, over-attribute the actions and performance of business organizations to their CEOs. Missing from this description is any recognition of the distinctive organizational and promotional dynamics that the celebrity industries share with the rest of what have been described as the cultural industries, or any mention of the ways these dynamics have been intensified by the fundamental changes that have occurred in the media sectors over the last few decades. These include deregulation, conglomeration, globalization, the proliferation of visual, digital, and online media channels, and the increasing convergence and interconnection of these various media platforms. Turner (2004), among others, insists that an understanding of these transformations is central to any account of the contemporary celebrity industries.

So one set of scholars neglects to consider business celebrities but provides a compelling analysis of the celebrity business. The other set of scholars takes up the subject of business celebrities but downplays the significance of the business dynamics that produce them. Our goal in this chapter is to bring these two bodies of work together, building on the insights offered by each perspective and hopefully avoiding their respective blind spots. We therefore provide a review of relevant research on celebrity, first in organization and management studies, then in cultural and media studies. We focus in particular on how research in these two disciplines describes the production of celebrity, because our understanding of these processes exerts considerable influence over how we understand the celebrities they produce. We emphasize that the celebrity industries exhibit in intensified form several of the defining characteristics of the cultural industries more generally, in particular the vital participation of a loosely coupled network of third parties, intermediaries, and promotional entrepreneurs. From this perspective, to maintain simply that journalists create business celebrities is to underplay a host of other factors (not least the active participation of many CEOs and their firms in the fame game), and to gloss over the fundamentally multivalent nature of the cultural icons that result from this complex relational process.

We define business celebrity as a cultural commodity produced by a distinctive industrial process. This process entails the orchestrated co-production, cross-promotion, and circulation of exemplary business personalities via a wide range of media platforms and channels. We understand this process from a production of culture perspective, which holds that "the symbolic elements of culture are shaped by the systems within which they are created, distributed, evaluated, taught, and preserved" (Peterson and Anand 2004: 311). In other words, the organizational logic and operating dynamics of that process contribute a great deal to the shape of the celebrities it produces. The products of the diffuse, relational, and often contentious process of celebrification are equally diffuse, relational, and contentious. The ranks of business celebrity include figures of various sorts who receive widespread and self-perpetuating media exposure. Media narratives and images of their actions, personalities, and / or private lives come to serve a very public function. They become sites of interaction and struggle over what it means to be an individual and to take action in a society dominated by business forces and institutions beyond individual control.

The romance of leadership and the social construction of business leaders in the popular press

Research on celebrity in organization and management studies begins with the investigation of what has been called the romance of leadership. While much of leadership research continues to seek out the internal psychological dynamics that supposedly make leaders great, a number of scholars have looked instead into why business leaders are so adamantly attributed with greatness and socially constructed as central to organizational performance (Calder 1977; Pfeffer 1977; Meindl *et al*. 1985; Chen and Meindl 1991; Khurana 2002a, 2002b; Hayward *et al*. 2004; Guthey and Jackson 2005). The strength of the existing research on business celebrity in management and organization studies lies precisely in this emphasis on processes of attribution and social construction. Meindl *et al*. prepared the groundwork for applying this emphasis to business celebrity with their landmark article on "The Romance of Leadership" (1985). They point out that "the social construction of organizational realities has elevated the concept of leadership to a lofty status and level of significance," investing the concept with "a brilliance that exceeds the limits of normal scientific inquiry" (1985: 78). Both observers and participants in organizational life have developed "highly romanticized, heroic views" of leaders and their significance, the authors maintain, constructing in the process an imagery and a mythology that attributes leaders with mysterious and near mystical powers.

Again, the notion of attribution is key here. Staw (1975) first suggested that what seem like cause–effect relationships between organizational events, actions, and actors may represent projections and inferences rather than actual instances of one thing determining another. Calder (1977) and Pfeffer (1977) first applied this notion of attribution to leadership. With a nod to Weick's (1979) emphasis on sense making, Meindl, Ehrlich, and Dukerich argue that such attribution processes are central to the ways that organizational actors and scholars make sense of events and occurrences. On this basis, they argue, "leadership is perhaps best construed as an explanatory category that can be used to explain and account for organizational activities and outcomes" (1985: 79). From this perspective the romance of leadership performs an adaptive function. Organizations are large and complex systems in which multiple and competing inputs and causal determinants exist in a constant state of flux. The necessity of making sense of this chaos leads to a biased preference for the kind of more simplified, accessible, and comforting explanatory framework that leadership can provide. "In the absence of direct, unambiguous information that would allow one rationally to infer the locus of causality," Meindl *et al*. conclude, "the romanticized conception of leadership permits us to be more comfortable in associating leaders—by ascribing to them control and responsibility—with events and outcomes to which they can be plausibly linked" (1985: 80).

Chen and Meindl (1991) elaborated on this idea, exploring the specific ways in which the business press contributes to the romance of leadership by constructing and disseminating images of leaders as heroic figures worthy of public attention. "These images feed and expand our appetites for leadership products," they observed, "appealing not only to our collective commitments to the concept but fixating us in particular on the personas and characteristics of leaders themselves." To test this hypothesis, they performed a content analysis of newspaper and magazine articles about People Express Airlines CEO Donald Burr, and surveyed seventy-five undergraduate business students who read the articles to determine the image of Burr that resulted. The ways that leadership images were constructed and adjusted to accommodate new events, they concluded, could be attributed to the particular constraints and pressures placed on journalists as they carried out their job. In their view the professional values of the news industry together with the organizational routinization of news reporting reinforce an antideterminist bias whereby journalists attribute the performance of business organizations to the actions of individual leaders rather than to organizational dynamics or external forces.

Chen and Meindl focused in particular on the ways that both the popular press and its readership end up developing commitments to these leadership attributions, to the point where new, negative performance information can cause cognitive dissonance and raise issues of legitimacy and accuracy in reporting. To avoid this problem, they found, the popular press and its readership responded to performance downturns by carefully reconstructing the image of the heroic leader in ways that did not diminish "the significance of leadership as a way of understanding performance." In their case study, for example, "the image of Burr over time achieved a certain consistency with the past at the same time that it was modified to accommodate new and radically different information regarding the fortunes of People Express." The preservation of the leadership concept remained of paramount concern to all parties in this process, they concluded, because "In doing so, we rescue ourselves from the threats of a dangerous and capricious world and the disconcerting prospects of uncontrollable, if organized, human systems."

Although this research did not mention the celebrity phenomenon specifically, many of the insights, terms, and concepts introduced by Meindl and his various co-authors can be used to explore what we might call "the romance of business celebrity." First of all, their emphasis on attribution and social construction is crucial for understanding business celebrity, and heavily influences our own understanding and definition thereof. Second, these scholars' emphasis on the centrality of the popular press to the social construction of romanticized images of leadership clearly informs our emphasis on the role of business culture intermediaries in the construction of business celebrity. As we discuss further below, however, it is important not to restrict our understanding of this role to print journalists alone. Third, Chen's and Meindl's mobilization of the distinction between determinism and anti-determinism is particularly useful. As we noted in the first chapter, the celebrity phenomenon pivots on the issue of individual agency in the face of vast social and economic forces that encroach upon the individual's ability to take effective action in the modern business world.

Finally, as Chen and Meindl stressed, and as we also noted in the first chapter, the fortunes of individuals socially constructed as celebrities can change rapidly, sometimes overnight, and often with almost monthly regularity. Given the fact that these authors performed most of this research on the romance of leadership before management studies first had developed a firm grasp of the phenomenon of management fashions (Abrahamson 1996; Huczynski 2007; Jackson 2001), their discussion of commitment and change over time was particularly prescient. There are many connections and similarities between the fortunes of business celebrities and the cycles of management fashion. For this reason, as we will discuss at several points later in this book, the research literature on the cycles of management fashion can help illuminate the cycles and dynamics of business celebrity, with respect to not only management gurus, but leaders and entrepreneurs as well.

The causes and consequences of CEO and firm celebrity

Recently, a small group of scholars has begun to apply the central ideas from the romance and social construction of leadership literature specifically to the phenomenon of CEO celebrity (Hayward *et al.* 2004; Rindova *et al.* 2006; Wade *et al.* 2006). Hayward *et al.* introduced this research with an article in the *Strategic Management Journal* entitled "Believing One's Own Press: The Causes and Consequences of CEO Celebrity" (2004). They begin with an effusive quote from a 1998 *Business Week* article that places Jack Welch at the forefront of the pantheon of laudable CEOs: "No one, not Microsoft's William H. Gates III or Intel's Andrew S. Grove, not Walt Disney's Michael D. Eisner or Berkshire Hathaway's Warren E. Buffet, not even the late Coca-Cola chieftain Roberto C. Goizueta or the late Wal-Mart founder Sam Walton has created more shareholder value than Jack Welch" (Byrne 1998). The quote exemplifies for Hayward, Rindova, and Pollock how journalists create celebrity CEOs. They therefore develop a theory of CEO celebrity "in order to explain how the tendency of journalists to attribute a firm's actions and outcomes to the volition of its CEO affects such a firm." Their main point is that journalists give too much credit to CEOs and too little credit to broader situational factors when reporting on firm performance, and that CEOs who internalize this romanticized estimation of their own abilities and significance risk acting on hubris and making decisions that may be less beneficial to the firm than to their own inflated sense of self-importance and celebrity.

To make this point the authors hearken back to the social psychological concept of the fundamental attribution error (Heider 1958: Ross 1988). According to this theory, individuals are more likely to seek to explain events by looking at stable explanatory factors, such as the personality of key actors involved, rather than fleeting circumstances or situational factors. "Our model suggests that journalists' work demands cause them to magnify the fundamental attribution error of over-attributing behavior to the actor's dispositional qualities," Hayward *et al.* state. "In the process of attributing a firm's actions and performance to its CEOs, journalists create 'celebrity CEOs'" (2004: 638). The authors also spell out several conditions that make it more likely for journalists to attribute CEOs with celebrity status. Leaders of larger firms are generally more likely to become celebrities, they argue, especially if the firm under his or her leadership takes distinctive action compared to other firms, and if the actions are consistent with other actions taken under the CEO's leadership in other situations or firms (Hayward *et al.* 2004: 641). The authors also propose that "the greater the availability of information about a CEO's idiosyncratic personal behaviors, the greater the likelihood that journalists will attribute a firm's strategic action(s) to its CEO" (2004: 643).

In "The Burden of Celebrity: The Impact of CEO Certification Contests on CEO Pay and Performance" (2006), Wade, Porac, Pollock, and Graffin combine the concept of CEO celebrity with the statistical analysis of executive compensation. They correlate the results from *Financial World* magazine's "CEO of the Year" contest to the compensation of the executives ranked high on the list. They found that CEOs anointed as stars received higher compensation than those who weren't when their firms performed well, but that the stars received lower compensation when firm performance was poor. They also found that, overall, certification as a star by the *Financial World* list led to lower compensation over the long term. This was the case, they concluded, because external markers of star status "may supplement traditional governance mechanisms by inducing attributions of competence that evolve into expectations for higher performance." Whether or not star

CEOs actually deserved their salaries, they pointed out, such external certifications make a big difference, because "boards of directors often believe that CEOs do great things that warrant high pay, and this perception rules the compensation-setting process." According to this research the ranking of CEO celebrities functions as a social device "invented at a collective level as a means to assess the abilities of actors by creating a competency ordering among them."

In "Celebrity Firms: The Social Construction of Market Popularity," Rindova, Pollock, and Hayward (2006) extend their understanding of celebrity from the individual to the firm level in order to explain why some companies seem to garner so much more media attention than others. They open the article with another extended quote, this time from an article in *Fortune* magazine, comparing the Enron Corporation to a gyrating, young Elvis Presley gate-crashing "a country-club dinner dance with a bunch of old fogies and their wives shuffling around halfheartedly to the not-so-stirring sounds of Guy Lombardo and his All-Tuxedo Orchestra" (O'Reilly 2000: 148, quoted in Rindova *et al.* 2006: 50). The authors define celebrity firms like Enron as "those firms that attract a high level of public attention and generate positive emotional responses from stakeholder audiences" (2006: 51). They maintain that such celebrity status at the firm level functions as an intangible asset similar to reputation, status, or legitimacy, because it influences stakeholders' perceptions and allows firms to reap benefits similar to those associated with individual celebrities.

Working from the model they developed with respect to celebrity CEOs, Rindova, Pollock, and Hayward maintain that such celebrity firms are created when journalists hold them up as examples of important business changes and broader social developments. "We argue that journalists often attribute extraordinary qualities to some firms and their actions and, in the process, endow these firms with celebrity" (2006: 50). But the concept of the fundamental attribution error turns out to be difficult to apply in their account of celebrity firms, because it is not exactly an error to attribute firm-level actions to a celebrity firm. For this reason the authors concentrate instead in this article on the way the media constructs what they call a "dramatized reality" around celebrity firms, drawing this latter concept from select research on media effects and the poetics of drama (Bryant and Miron 2002; Zillmann 1994; both quoted in Rindova *et al.* 2006). If firms take bold or unusual actions or exhibit a distinctive identity, the authors argue, it becomes even more likely that the media will seize upon them to construct such a "dramatized reality" (2006: 55).

Perspectives from cultural and media studies

The organization and management scholars discussed above approach celebrity in a very different manner than the scholars who have paid the most attention to it. These latter work primarily under the interdisciplinary umbrella of cultural and media studies. Rindova, Pollock, and Hayward cite one important contribution to this body of work, Gamson's *Claims to Fame: Celebrity in Contemporary America* (1994), to argue that very little research has been done on celebrity at all. But this statement glosses over the wealth of research produced by cultural and media studies scholars in the decade between the publication of Gamson's book and their own contribution. This research includes several other substantial books: Marshall's *Celebrity and Power* (1997), Turner, Bonner, and Marshall's *Fame Games: The Production of Celebrity in Australia* (2000), Rojek's *Celebrity* (2001), Turner's *Understanding Celebrity* (2004), and Evans and Hesmondhalgh's *Understanding Media: Inside Celebrity* (2005). Even Gamson's book, which Rindova, Pollock, and Hayward do cite, looks very different when considered in the broader context of cultural studies research on celebrity, rather than from the narrower confines of a focus on social psychological processes of attribution.

With a small number of significant exceptions in the sub-discipline of critical management studies (for example Du Gay 1996; Parker 2006), organization and management scholars have made very little use of perspectives from cultural studies. This is understandable given the fact that cultural studies is so hard to pin down, consisting as it does of a loosely structured blend of sociology and social theory, political economy and Marxist theory, history, semiotics and literary theory, film and media studies, and cultural anthropology. But Marshall (1997) argues that the complexity of celebrity defies any simple or linear analysis, and calls for an interdisciplinary set of conceptual tools that can juggle a variety of often competing and contradictory symbolic, interpretive, cultural, ideological, and commercial factors. From this perspective it makes sense that scholars of cultural and media studies approach celebrity from an eclectic mix of methodological and theoretical perspectives, exploring celebrity as commodity, as sign, as text, as image, as persona, as ideology, as industry, and as negotiated celebration. While difficult to synthesize, then, approaches to celebrity in cultural and media studies are appropriate to the complexity of the topic at hand.

Another possible reason that organization and management research does not incorporate many insights from cultural studies is that this latter field has drawn heavily from a Marxist and neo-materialist tradition that can seem very alien to scholars working primarily in business schools. This heritage is reflected strongly in the interest on the part of many cultural studies scholars in the notion of hegemony, which Lash argues functioned as "the concept that de facto crystallized cultural studies as a discipline" (2007: 55). Drawing on the work of Gramsci, cultural studies scholars have defined hegemony as the manner in which the ruling capitalist order dominates society by means of the consent of the dominated, employing ideology, discourse, popular culture, and symbolic power as much as direct force or coercion. Scholars connected to the so-called Frankfurt School in the 1930s and 1940s developed this idea into a critique of the way that the culture industries produced celebrities and other cultural commodities in order to deceive the masses and distract them from the true sources of inequality in capitalist society. As Marshall paraphrases their argument, Frankfurt School critics maintained that "the masses are by their very nature psychologically immature and thus are drawn to the magic of these larger-than-life personalities in the same way children identify with and implicitly trust their parents" (1997: 9).

A countervailing tradition in cultural studies, one that became particularly prominent in the 1980s and 1990s, sought to refute the rather condescending overtones of this "manipulation thesis" by championing the ability of the supposedly dominated classes to resist cultural hegemony and subvert dominant ideologies by means of the creative consumption and appropriation of commodities and cultural products towards countercultural ends (see, for example, Ross 1988). While this perspective eventually came under criticism for over-romanticizing the agency of those excluded from mainstream sources of power, it convincingly drove home the point that consumers are not cultural dupes who merely swallow undigested what the media or the cultural industries serve up to them. The continuing debate between these two broad tendencies provides cultural studies with the closest thing the field has to a central unifying concept, with the result that many cultural studies scholars describe culture as a terrain of negotiation and conflict between hegemonic forces and grassroots forms of resistance. Hall, for example, describes popular culture as "one of the sites where this struggle for and against a culture of the powerful is engaged," and as "the arena of consent and resistance" (1981: 228, quoted in Marshall 1997: 45). "Popular culture always is part of power relations," concurs Fiske. "It always bears traces of the constant struggle between domination and subordination, between power and various forms of resistance to it or evasions of it (1989: 19, quoted in Marshall 1997: 45).

Small wonder, then, that cultural studies scholars have seized upon the topic of celebrity, which brings to the fore these issues of power, individual agency and consumption in the context of cultural production and consumption. These interests, combined with the disciplinary heritage described above, have led cultural studies scholars to pursue research on celebrity in two general and often overlapping directions. One strand of research delivers a broad cultural critique of the way that celebrity functions in consumer capitalism, while the other concentrates more specifically on the economic and organizational dynamics of the cultural industries that produce celebrities. Our aim is to review both of these aspects of research on celebrity in cultural studies, and to combine insights from both in order to develop a better understanding of the nature of business celebrity.

Critiquing celebrity culture

Rojek's *Celebrity* (2001) exemplifies how many scholars channel the interests and influences that have defined cultural studies in the direction of a sweeping critique of consumer capitalism. He links the phenomenon of celebrity directly to the central logic of commodity capitalism itself, arguing that celebrity culture functions as a key mechanism for mobilizing the abstract consumer desire required to move ever more new goods and keep the economic system functioning (2001: 187ff.). Rojek defines celebrity as "the attribution of glamorous or notorious status to an individual within the public sphere" by means of the process of "celebrification." The "cultural fabrications" that result from this process are more than just persons of renown, a term which Rojek defines as "the informal attribution of distinction on an individual within a given social network" (2001: 12). The key distinction for Rojek is that celebrification occurs via the media, at a distance, and it generates what he describes as an abstract form of consumer desire. Abstract consumer desire can never really be fulfilled regardless of whether one obtains this or that concrete object of desire, he explains, a state of affairs which the market system requires in order to allow for the perpetual demand for new goods. Celebrities are better at mobilizing this sort of desire than concrete objects, Rojek continues, because celebrity "embodies desire in an animate object, which allows for deeper levels of attachment and identification than with inanimate commodities." Moreover, he argues, "celebrities can be reinvented to renew desire, and because of this they are extremely efficient resources in the mobilization of global desire" (2001: 189).

Rojek's approach allows him to account for an aspect of celebrity missing from the research in organization and management studies described above— that is, the intense levels of devotion and emotional attachment celebrities can generate among large numbers of fans. In many instances the abstract desire generated by celebrity can involve "emotional, sexual, spiritual and existential identification with the celebrity," he points out. It is from the basis of this recognition that he launches his trenchant critique of the celebrity system. "The passion that fans feel for celebrities is not merely a matter of cherishing the technical accomplishments or the aesthetic public face of the celebrity," he argues. "In mobilizing desire for the celebrity, fans are also articulating a lack in themselves and in the culture around them" (2001: 196). At certain points in his argument, as we discuss in Chapter 5, Rojek connects this sense of absence or lack to the decline of organized religion. But he also attributes it to the manner in which consumer capitalism makes it impossible for consumers to fulfill their desires to connect with or even become like celebrities. On the one hand, the news and entertainment media that provide access to celebrities also function to keep them at a distance. On the other, fans are often very conscious of the fact that the idealized public face of the celebrity is a construction, and that direct contact with the private, or veridical self of the celebrity would not necessarily fulfill their abstract desires anyway. In extreme cases, Rojek points out, "this can lead to hopeless and painful feelings of resignation when the imaginary relationship with the celebrity is unconsummated, or to aggressive feelings of resentment against the celebrity" (2001: 196). Rojek concludes that "in building up strong receptivity to celebrity and commodity culture, capitalism and democracy produce weakly integrated personalities who are vulnerable to external attraction and its vagaries" (2001: 197). Such statements highlight the manner in which his approach approximates a contemporary version of the Frankfurt School's manipulation thesis whereby the power of celebrity culture overwhelms the psychologically weak individual.

As the very title of Marshall's *Celebrity and Power* (1997) makes clear, his cultural critique of celebrity also foregrounds issues of power. But Marshall manages to paint a more balanced picture of the way that audiences can respond to celebrity as something more than cultural dupes. Marshall defines celebrities as "public personalities" who function to provide a forum or a platform for working out the meaning of individual and collective identity in contemporary society. He begins from the simple observation that the media treat celebrities as being very special and very different from the rest of the population. In Marshall's words, these individuals "are given greater presence, and a wider scope of activity and agency than are those who make up the rest of the population." While celebrities gain stature from the manner in which the media portray them as individuals who are more powerful than the rest of us, Marshall argues the true nature of celebrity power derives from the way they represent individuality itself, and the way they provide ideal examples of how it is even possible to be an individual and take action in a society dominated by collective economic and social forces beyond any one person's control. "The power of celebrity, then, is to represent the active construction of identity in the social world," explains Marshall. "Studying the celebrity offers the reader of culture a privileged view of the representative forms of modern subjectivity that pass through the celebrity discourses." Marshall therefore describes celebrities as "stand-ins" or surrogates for the idea that all individuals in society can take action and make a difference in the social world. In this regard he echoes Dyers' argument that film stars "articulate what it is to be a human being in contemporary society" (1986: 8, quoted in Turner 2004: 103). Among other things, Marshall argues, this helps explain why so many celebrities become activists and spokespersons for political, environmental, and social causes (1997: 244).

But Marshall is careful to stress that the power of celebrity is not overtly political. Rather he characterizes it as "affective," by which he means that celebrity culture exerts its power by reducing political, social, and economic forces to a matter of personality, psychological motivations, and personal feelings. "The celebrity is the avant-garde of this movement to vivisect public action by identifying the original private experience," says Marshall. "It functions as a discursive vehicle that reduces the cultural meaning of events, incidents and people to their psychological makeup" (1997: 247). Turner supports this argument when he observes that the "precise moment a public figure becomes a celebrity" occurs when his or her private life begins to achieve just as much attention as any public role or achievement (2004: 8). Celebrity culture achieves this transformation by recasting personality and the private sphere as "the ultimate site of truth and meaning for any representation in the public sphere." Unlike Rojek, who views celebrity as indicative of the split between public personalities and the private self, Marshall therefore maintains that celebrities represent the "disintegration of the distinction between the private and the public" (1997: 247). The relentless manner in which celebrity culture mobilizes private "revelations" towards public purposes renders the two spheres nearly indistinguishable from one another.

For this reason Marshall does not conclude along with Rojek that celebrity culture inevitably produces weakly integrated personalities who cannot withstand the attractions and ideological subtexts offered up by celebrity culture. Granted, celebrities are produced by a commodity system that reflects the interests of the most dominant groups and forces in the capitalist society. But he stresses that the meanings generated on the basis of these productions have to come from the audience, and that in order for a celebrity to gain any traction, audience members must "actively work on the presentation of the celebrity in order to make it fit their everyday experiences" (1997: 47). The ability to actively participate in the construction of celebrity is a form of audience power. In taking this position, Marshall therefore reflects the influence of the cultural studies approach summarized above, and exemplified by the work of Hall and Fiske. From this perspective, celebrity functions as a site of constant negotiation and struggle over the nature of individual agency and collective identity in modern society. "The celebrity is simultaneously a construction of the dominant culture and a construction of the subordinate audiences of the culture," he argues. "These conceptions of the celebrity, those arising from below . . . and those emerging from above . . . never entirely merge into one coherent form of celebrity identity" (1997: 48). It follows that celebrities can have multiple, even competing identities and serve many different functions in the service of many different interests. As we will make clear in the next section, an analysis of the organization of the celebrity industries supports this point of view.

The industrial dynamics of celebrity production

The problem with sweeping theoretical critiques of the sort reviewed above is that they can contribute to the impression that abstract cultural forces themselves exert agency, determine people's actions, and cause things to happen in the realm of everyday experience—in this instance, that they can give rise to celebrity. But research in cultural studies also emphasizes the importance of everyday activities and lived experience. From this perspective a number of cultural studies scholars have explored how celebrity results from an often chaotic accumulation of individual interests, organizational decisions, promotional activities, representational practices, and commercial transactions, along with a fair amount of sheer luck or happenstance. These activities are not totally random, but neither are they predetermined by the heavy hand of some monolithic guiding force like "the media," "capitalism," or "consumer desire." The complex network of intersecting players and practices that produce celebrity gives a distinctive shape and logic to what we have referred to as the celebrity industries.

Gamson argues that it is not entirely inappropriate to describe the production of celebrity with the language normally reserved for the mass production of factory goods. "Those working within it speak primarily in the language of commerce and machinery," he observes. "They are organized industrially, with production tasks divided between tightly linked sub industries; marketing plays a key role in matching products to distributors and consumers, depending especially on strategies of product transformation and the building of consumer loyalty" (1994: 58). But Gamson is also quick to point out that there are significant differences between celebrity production and the commodity production of more conventional consumer goods. We can account for these differences by emphasizing the fact that the celebrity industries form part of what have been termed the cultural industries (Hirsch 1972; Lampel *et al.* 2000).

Jones and Thornton describe the cultural industries as "those organizations that design, produce, and distribute products that appeal to aesthetic or expressive tastes more than to the utilitarian aspects of customer needs such as films, books, building designs, fashion, and music" (2005: xi). These industries are driven by creative workers and organized around knowledge and aesthetics, Jones and Thornton point out, and they "create products that serve important symbolic functions such as capturing, refracting, and legitimating societal knowledge and values" (Ibid.). According to Hirsch (1972), such industries are organized in a very distinctive way because of the many uncertainties they face. Many of these uncertainties stem from the fact that it is impossible to predict in advance which cultural products will appeal to consumer or audience tastes and preferences and which will fall flat. This problem is exacerbated by the impossibility of knowing whether a variety of "mass-media gatekeepers"—journalists, critics, and so on—will provide the coverage and exposure needed to allow a particular product to catch on. To mitigate these uncertainties, Hirsch argues, the cultural industries include many entrepreneurial individuals and organizations in the production process, and they use many "boundary spanners" and "intelligence agents" to try to anticipate and influence the decisions of media and industry gatekeepers. Ironically, of course, the involvement of all of these people in the production process leads to further uncertainty.

Even among these already distinctive industries, several aspects of the celebrity industries make them stand out as particularly unique, and make them somewhat difficult to analyze as well. As Gamson points out, for example, celebrities themselves function at one and the same time as central members of the workforce and as the main product for sale (1994: 63). We can add to this the observation that the production of celebrities is synonymous with the promotion thereof. As if this were not confusing enough, Turner further points out that the rest of the key players in these industries work very hard to hide or mask any trace of the contribution of their labor to these processes of production and promotion. "By presenting publicity as news, by claiming to tell us what their charges 'are really like,' by managing the production of 'candid' photo opportunities and so on, the celebrity industries work hard to naturalize their professional practices—or else to submerge their professional practices beneath those of another profession, such as journalism," says Turner. "As a result, what these industries do is not easy to distinguish and therefore their importance is not easy to assess" (2004: 41).

Another complicating factor is the manner in which the production of celebrities spans a number of different industries or sub-industries. Rein, Kotler, and Stoller include in this list the entertainment industry, the communications industry, the publicity industry, the representation industry, the appearance industry, the coaching industry, and the endorsement industry (1987). "We don't need to accept these categories," remarks Turner, "but they do give us a good overview of the range of cultural intermediaries required to make this system function" (2004: 42). These are Hirsch's intelligence agents and boundary spanners, a loosely coupled network of corporate representatives, cultural entrepreneurs, and third-party go-betweens that includes talent agents, managers, publicists, marketers and advertising executives, public relations departments, newspaper editors and journalists, television producers, book publishers, talk-show hosts, photographers, stylists, bloggers, and many others. The term Turner uses to describe these various players—cultural intermediaries—is a significant one. It was first introduced by Bourdieu (1984) to refer to a new petit bourgeois class of service and knowledge workers central to "occupations involving presentation and representation . . . providing symbolic goods and services" (Bourdieu 1984: 359, quoted in Negus 2002: 502). According to Negus, the notion of cultural intermediaries emphasizes the activities of those workers who mediate between the producers of cultural products and the consumers thereof. "This is a significant shift from transmission models of cultural production whereby various writers have portrayed the aesthetic economy in terms of analogies with assembly lines, or 'filter flow' systems, tracing the movement of 'raw materials' from creative artist to consumer" (2002: 503).

This is precisely the point that prompts Gamson to distinguish between traditional factory modes of production and the working logic of the celebrity industries. The fact that the latter is marked by the activities of so many different cultural intermediaries means that it is thoroughly decentralized, characterized by networks of relationships and interconnections rather than vertical integration and streamlined throughput. Turner maintains that these connections and relationships are the key to understanding the way celebrity is produced. "The most obvious connections are corporate: such as, when we find that *Time* magazine is featuring a story on an actor who is currently appearing in a film produced by Warner Bros," Turner points out. "But there are others: strong social, cultural and professional networks see individuals move easily from one side of the industrial divide to the other—reporters become press officers, journalists become public relations advisers and so on." Again, because they involve the individual career trajectories of many different behind-the-scenes players, these relationships are often very difficult to see. Turner goes so far as to argue that they are "deliberately mystified . . . so that the processes through which they work . . . are not visible" (2004: 45).

Even if the majority of relationships that keep the celebrity industries running are not always readily visible, it is evident that they are not all cooperative. "Although the workers in the various celebrity-producing industries are in many ways tightly allied, the relationships among those actively producing celebrity representations also pull in a variety of directions," observes Gamson. Depending on their organizational affiliation or business plan, these different actors can have very different interests and very different ideas about how the celebrities in their charge should appear. Some are involved in selling the celebrity *per se*, while others are interested in using the celebrity to hawk other goods. "Key players with short-term interests tend to emphasize a performer's vehicles over her career," observes Gamson, "while players with long-term interests will emphasize career over vehicle" (1994: 81). Some players in the industry have no use for celebrities who are too famous or garner too much fan loyalty, and others make it their job to tear celebrities down by publicizing or trumping up rumors or scandals. For all of these reasons, Gamson characterizes the celebrity industries as "the scene of constant battles for control" (1994: 85). He explains:

> The most central ones, guided by the variety of interests already described, are struggles for control of the commodification process, the direction and content of the attended-to: Who gets to decide what the celebrity will look like, what she will talk about and with whom? Who, finally, gets to produce the commodity for profit? Because the celebrity has so many producers, the industry so many subsidiaries, the answer is ambiguous and contested. Parties persuade, cajole, and flatter each other: they barter and trade; when all else fails, they battle.
>
> (Gamson 1994: 85)

Many of these battles revolve around issues of access. The number of interdependencies and third parties involved in the celebrity production process gives rise to a preponderance of gatekeepers who can gain power by restricting or blocking access to important resources or connections. As Gamson explains, gatekeeping is absolutely central to the celebrity industries because the main attraction on offer is the proverbial peek behind the curtain of fame at the "true story" and the "real person." "To be competitive in the marketplace, many programs and publications promise audiences something they cannot get elsewhere: the exclusive, inside story, a look at the 'reality' behind the image," observes Gamson (1994: 92). This is equally true of the coverage of business celebrities. For example, the celebrity profile that ran as a *Time* magazine cover story during the height of the Microsoft antitrust trial was titled "In Search of the Real Bill Gates." The article opened with the following words:

> He's the most famous businessman in the world. Reams have been written about how he dominated the revolution in personal computing and is now poised to turn Microsoft into a media and Internet behemoth. But we know little about him as a person. What beliefs and values drive this man who, as much as anyone, will determine the way we look not only at computers but at ourselves and our world? Here's an intimate look at one of the most important minds and personalities of our era.
>
> (Isaacson 1997: 44)

The illusion of intimacy here depends crucially on the appearance of access to the "backstage" of Bill Gates' private life. Because relationships and connections in the celebrity system are in Gamson's phrase "deliberately mystified," it would be very difficult to prove that the negative publicity generated by the antitrust trial prompted Gates' public relations advisors to grant the *Time* reporters extensive access to this backstage in order to humanize Gates' image at a crucial time. But this is precisely the point—the reporters *had to be granted access*, because access to celebrities like Gates is a precious commodity controlled by public relations professionals and other business culture intermediaries. "The celebrity and the publicist know the value of the information commodity, and they control its scarcity to maintain its value in extracting exposure," Gamson points out (1994: 92). This is a source of considerable power, one that levels the playing field between public relations professionals and journalists. "The more dependent a magazine or program is on celebrity images for sales . . . the more powerless they are to make editorial evaluations and control content," Gamson explains further, because "cutting oneself off from publicists means cutting oneself off from the main pipeline to celebrity interviews and information" (1994: 90).

Such power struggles over access have governed the relationships between the news media and public relations professionals since the early twentieth century, but these tensions have been exacerbated in the last several decades by a number of fundamental changes in the media sectors that have influenced both journalistic practice and the dynamics of celebrity building (Turner 2004). These include deregulation, conglomeration, globalization, the proliferation of visual, digital, and online media channels, and the increasing convergence and interconnection of these various media platforms. More than ever before, the information-gathering and reporting functions of the news media have become thoroughly intertwined with the commercial and promotional logic of the media industries. At the same time, the proliferation of new media channels and technologies has provided opportunities for many alternative voices and viewpoints to influence the news process. News about organizational activities is often both initiated and shaped by a variety of cultural intermediaries other than traditionally conceived print journalists—talent agents, managers, publicists, marketers, public relations departments, television executives, book publishers, talk-show hosts, photographers, bloggers, and many others, all of which interact across different media platforms. Any account of celebrity that downplays the significance of these overlapping networks—and that over-attributes the creation of celebrity to the influence of print journalists alone—cannot account for the manner in which the celebrity industries perform their powerful promotional magic, including the manner in which they create business celebrities (Turner 2004: 47).

The relational dynamics of business celebrity

We have spent a considerable amount of time outlining the unique organizational dynamics of celebrity production because they are crucial for understanding the cultural and representational dynamics of what results from the process. The construction and promotion of celebrities is carried out not by any one sector or set of actors, such as journalists, but by a variety of loosely coupled third parties and intermediaries who work at cross-purposes as often as they collaborate. The cognitive mechanisms employed by print journalists to make sense of firm activities certainly have an important role to play in this process, but they are only one part of a much larger and more complex set of activities. These include four different kinds of social or relational dynamics that contribute to the process of celebrification. The dynamics of *attribution* highlighted by organization and management scholars are central to the construction of business celebrities, but they mean little apart from the dynamics of *access* to the celebrity him or herself. These issues of access also highlight the importance of the dynamics of *mediation* to the construction of celebrity—by which term we refer to the crucial shaping role played by a number of individuals, organizations, and institutions acting as promotional agents, boundary spanners, and gatekeepers. One final dynamic that is essential for the construction of celebrity has been implicit in our discussion up to this point. In order for all these elements to crystallize into the phenomenon we call celebrity, the individual in question has to obtain what we might call, for lack of a better word, *traction* among these many different parties, and among media consumers as well. That is, the burgeoning celebrity needs to find a foothold at different points all along the celebrification process by appealing to many different and often conflict-ing interests and agendas all at once. To coin a phrase from Walt Whitman, celebrities must contain multitudes. For this reason, they must contain many contradictions, debates, and tensions as well.

With these relational dynamics in mind, we can restate and elaborate on the definition of business celebrities we introduced in the previous chapter. As our discussion has made abundantly clear, they are not simply well-known individuals who are attributed by journalists with actions or characteristics that lead to or exemplify business success. They are best understood as clusters of promotional activities, representational practices, and cultural dynamics that revolve around different types of exemplary business personalities—corporate leaders, entrepreneurs, management gurus, investment bankers, traders, marketers, Hollywood agents and producers, and so on. From this perspective business celebrity consists of the orchestrated co-production, cross-promotion, and circulation of images, narratives, and personal appear-ances of such figures via a wide range of media platforms and channels. As a result of these practices, candidates for celebrity are given widespread exposure in the media to the point where, if conditions are right and they gain enough traction, their individual actions, personal traits, physical presence, and/or private lives come to serve multiple and interconnected promotional and cultural/ideological functions in ways that reinforce their celebrity status.

Our definition echoes Abrahamson's treatment of management fashions by emphasizing both a process—celebrification—and its outcome—business celebrities (Abrahamson 1996). It follows that business figures who merely become well known or highly visible in the media are not necessarily celebrities. We reserve this label for products of a process of "celebrification" dominated by the promotional activities of business culture intermediaries connected to the celebrity industries. We make this point to emphasize that celebrity does not simply occur naturally, even to deserving individuals, nor does it result from some universal human propensity to employ a particular set of cognitive mechanisms to make sense of experience. Business celebrity is an institution or system that requires the sustained efforts and cooperation of many people for its constant production, reproduction, and maintenance. Furthermore, this system serves a wide range of purposes, agendas, and interests—personal gain, entertainment, and diversion, obviously, but also promotional purposes, commercial, institutional, and organizational purposes, political, ideological, and cultural purposes, social, moral, and psychological purposes.

In Figure 2.1 we map out the relational dynamics of business celebrity, using as an example the case of the celebrity CEO. We intend for this diagram to highlight the dynamics of attribution, access, mediation, and traction we have discussed in this chapter by depicting the many players involved in the process of celebrification, and the multiple interactions that take place between them. Towards this end we have represented the various players involved in the production with multiple boxes, and with arrows between them to signify interaction, collaboration, and potential conflict with respect to production, promotion, and consumption. By this means we have sought to convey clearly that media consumers, for example, cannot be considered *en masse*. There are multiple consumers with different interests, views, and estimations of any given business celebrity. These consumers interact with each other and, via interpretation, appropriation, and response, with the media representations of the celebrity as well. By the same token we have sought to convey the idea that celebrities are not coherent or unitary figures—they consist of multiple images, narratives, and events that interact with and sometimes contradict each other. The spheres we have labeled "business culture intermediaries" and "organization" are also characterized by multiple interests and actors, as well as interaction or even conflict between them.

Significantly, we have not placed the CEO at the center of the diagram—that place of prominence belongs to the many business culture intermediaries that dominate the process as agents, go-betweens, and gatekeepers. Hence media consumers have no access to the celebrified CEO except via the news media and the promotional efforts of other intermediaries. The business

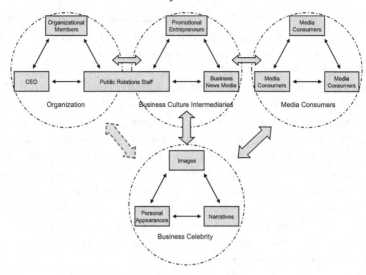

Figure 2.1 The dynamics of celebrification: the example of CEO celebrities.

news media themselves can only gain access to the CEO by dealing with his or her public relations representatives and agents. But neither do CEOs have full access to or control over their own celebrity status without the mediating intervention of a variety of public relations professionals and media gate-keepers. We placed a dotted line between the organization and the celebrity construct in order to convey the notion that there is some direct input—for example in the instance of personal appearances—and that CEOs and their organizations also constitute audiences or consumers of celebrity images, narratives, and appearances.

The picture we have drawn of the construction of business celebrities heavily influences our understanding of their broader cultural significance. As we stated in the previous chapter, the networked and heterarchical organ-ization of the celebrity system, along with the multiple interests and agendas it serves, have the effect of both highlighting and blurring the boundaries between several spheres of experience which we normally consider separate and distinct—including private/public, non-commercial/commercial, individual/social, cultural/psychological, and staged/authentic spheres. The central distinction that is both highlighted and erased by celebrity is that between individual agency on the one hand and collective or social agency on the other. Celebrities depend for their status as such on the activities of a complex network of individuals, organizations, commercial forces, and cultural dynamics, but in the process of celebrification and mediation these various activities get folded into or overshadowed by the personalities and actions of the celebrities themselves. As a result celebrities come to represent the possibility and desirability of untrammeled individual agency, power, and distinction in a complex world. In this sense business celebrity does indeed serve a sense-making function by providing a means for attributing corporate activities to individual agents. But largely as a result of the many inputs and conflicts that go into its production, business celebrity functions more fundamentally as a forum for ongoing dialogues and debates about what it means to be an individual in a corporate society in the first place. A workable definition needs to recognize this fundamentally dialogic nature of the celebrity figure, and recognize as well that different kinds of business celebrities frame these debates in different ways.

In the remainder of this book we explore these relational dynamics by looking more closely at two significant kinds of business celebrities—management gurus and celebrity CEOs—and by exploring various aspects of the celebrification process that invests these figures with their larger-than-life, but often fleeting status. In the next chapter we draw on Timothy Clark's and David Greatbatch's previous research on the staging of management guru events and the publication of management gurus' best-selling books to provide a vivid example of the crowded, interactive nature of the process that generates business celebrities. In subsequent chapters, we shift our gaze to the construction of another kind of business celebrities—high-profile CEOs and other top executives. In both instances, as we will demonstrate, an understanding of the celebrification process as we have described it in this chapter helps make sense of the many actors and activities that are necessary to bring about the orchestrated co-production of both management gurus and CEO celebrities.

3 Management gurus as management fashion celebrities

In the previous chapter we presented a model for understanding business celebrities that emphasizes the crowded nature of the celebrification process, the central roles played by the many actors and intermediaries who populate the celebrity industries, and the equally crucial contributions of media audiences to the manner in which business celebrities are produced, consumed, and understood. We stressed that constant interaction among these different players shapes the nature of the celebrities they all help produce. As a result, business celebrities are not merely exemplary individuals. They are also sites of debate and even conflict over what it means to be an individual in a society dominated by large corporations and other business institutions. But as we also pointed out, many of the intermediaries involved in the process of celebrification work hard to conceal or minimize their contributions in order to direct as much attention as possible towards the celebrities themselves. The irony of the business celebrity system is that it takes the efforts of so many people to reinforce the idea that certain gifted individuals dominate the world of business.

In this chapter we provide a vivid example of this irony by looking closely at those business celebrities attributed with generating and disseminating popular management ideas and fashions. Management gurus like Tom Peters, Stephen Covey, Rosabeth Moss Kanter, and Peter Senge gain widespread visibility and become well known through a variety of international public-speaking activities, best-selling books, media appearances, syndicated newspaper columns, DVDs, training programs, and consulting activities. In these various contexts they function as the most visible proselytizers of management ideas, to the point where the media constantly turn to such figures for authoritative commentary on the current and future state of the contemporary corporation (Clark and Salaman 1998; Suddaby and Greenwood 2001). They are often called upon to speak (for considerable fees) at key industry and intergovernmental conferences, and sometimes even to advise national government leaders.

The two activities that contribute most to the prominence and legitimacy of management gurus are their live appearances on the international lecture circuit, and the publication of best-selling books bearing their name. Both of these aspects of the management guru phenomenon exemplify the central irony of business celebrity as we have described it. Take, for example, live events featuring appearances by management gurus. These are most often staged as corporate extravaganzas, exciting events during which participants find inspiration in messages that can either reinforce or challenge their taken-for-granted assumptions about the nature of managerial activity and their own position and role in it. As Turner, Bonner, and Marshall (2000) point out, the organization of such events has become big business, and "every city sees it as a necessity to have a modern convention centre to handle this part of the tourist business, and every hotel is partly organized around facilities that appeal to corporate conferences" (p. 73). But in the event itself, all back-stage elements and manoeuvres function together to direct attention away from themselves and towards the charismatic presence of the guru him- or herself.

Such is the power of these events that they can work their magic even on someone who has studied them closely. For example, here is co-author Timothy Clark's personal recollection of his experience at an event featuring mega-gurus Charles Handy, Gary Hamel, and Michael Porter:

> I exited from the comfort and warmth of an international conference centre. Although I had become familiar with this area of the city in the last few days I was slightly disoriented and took a wrong turn to the train station. This was probably related to the fact that I had spent the day listening to nearly six hours of lectures by various management gurus. It had been an intense and engrossing day. Instead of thinking about the journey home or turning my mobile phone on to check voice and text messages, my mind was elsewhere. I was preoccupied with replaying a selection of segments from the different speeches I heard that day. My head was swirling with snippets, stories and quotations from the day. I was keen to get home and find the internet site of an apparently innovative supermarket chain. I started to think about whether my employer had a clear idea about its strategy? What could we do that was truly innovative and might outsmart our competitors? How could we redefine our market?

As I sat in the train carriage on my way home and these various thoughts circulated in my head I realised that I had become inhabited by the very ideas and language that I was researching. There I was, a management researcher, conducting a participant observation study of management gurus' lectures, supposedly capable of remaining separate from the events I was observing. Like many other people who attended, indiscernibly I had been drawn into the speakers' world. For this short journey at least, their words, stories and priorities fully occupied my thoughts.

Even someone familiar with how management guru lectures are staged and constructed for maximum effect can get caught up in the enthusiasm they generate. Something very personal can happen at such events, something akin to a transformation. For this reason many have argued that management gurus serve a quasi-religious function that revolves around the types of personal "conversion" experiences described above (Huczynski 2007; Clark and Salaman 1996; Greatbatch and Clark 2005). The connotations of the term "guru" in the context of eastern religious mysticism help to reinforce this view, and raise a set of critical questions about exactly who management gurus are and exactly what function they serve. The extent to which we can understand what happens in gurus' lectures in quasi-religious terms has a considerable bearing on how we understand management gurus themselves.

In the first part of this chapter we take this idea very seriously, drawing on Rojek's argument about the religious aspects of the celebrity phenomenon and the liminal experiences they can induce in their followers. Rojek (2001: 98) argues that "the rites of ascent and descent that were originally developed in primitive religion have been taken over and recast by celebrity culture." Building on the work of the anthropologist Eliade (1964) he argues that just like the shaman of earlier times the celebrity is able to conjure up powerful feelings that take fans on ecstatic journeys of ascent, descent, and rebirth. Such a view has been very prominent in academic discussions of management gurus. From this perspective such figures appear as quasi-evangelical speakers whose performances display many of the features of a shaman or witchdoctor.

The problem with this view is that it reinforces the intense and exclusive focus on the gurus and their powers upon which these events depend for their desired effect. Their role and status are foregrounded to the extent that everything that occurs at these events is presented as arising exclusively from the gurus' inspirational presence, insights, and actions. If, however, we broaden our focus to include the business of arranging guru lectures, a very different picture emerges. It becomes abundantly clear that the gurus are not solely responsible for the experiences produced at the event. Many third parties and intermediaries play crucial backstage roles in promoting and coordinating the event as a whole. From this perspective management guru lectures are orchestrated co-productions, and gurus themselves are better understood as *management fashion celebrities* subject to the dynamics of the celebrity industry we have described in previous chapters.

In the second half of this chapter we support this argument further by paying close attention to the crowded industrial process behind the production of business best-sellers. The names and images of management gurus feature prominently on the sort of books that overpopulate the business sections of airport bookstores the world over. Our interviews with editors and publishers of such books, as well as with some management gurus, make clear that in some instances, the gurus themselves have very little to do with actually writing what's inside them, or even coming up with the central ideas in the first place. The celebrity status of the "author" is of course crucial to the promotion of the book, and often to the marketing of a number of ancillary products connected to it. But in this sense the management fashion celebrity functions more like a brand than an author. Besides, publishers have plenty of ghost-writers on hand that can do the heavy lifting required to actually write a best-selling management book. Management gurus depend for their prominence on a web of cooperative arrangements and relationships that all function to make it look like the guru him- or herself makes all the magic happen. As with the celebrity phenomenon more generally, neither their inspirational public appearances nor their best-selling management books can be understood without reference to the many backstage workers and intermediaries whose activities, in effect, make them the business celebrities that they are.

Management gurus as management fashion celebrities

In Chapter 2 we have already alluded to the connections between the literature on celebrity and management fashion. In recent years there has been increasing interest in the notion that management ideas, methods, and techniques are subject to the same vagaries of fashion as aesthetic aspects of life such as clothing styles, hair length, musical genres, interior design, and house design. In Blumer's words management and organizations represent further social arenas within which "certain social forms enjoy temporary acceptance and respectability only to be replaced by others more abreast of the times" (1968: 342). There is therefore a constant churning of management ideas and techniques as some attract a broad-based following only for the initial enthusiasm to diminish after a period and for other ideas and techniques to succeed them as the focal point of popular attention. In a study of sixteen fashionable ideas over five decades Carson *et al.* (2000: 1152) show that the period of time between the introduction of a fashionable management idea or technique and the peak in its popularity fell from a mean of 14.8 years in the 1950s–1970s, to 7.5 years in the 1980s, to 2.6 years in the 1990s. This study suggests that during this forty-year time period the peaks for fashionable management ideas became higher while their lifespans decreased in length. It would be interesting to compare these figures to the ever-shorter lifespan of business celebrities, and media celebrities more generally as well.

Building on this notion of temporariness, researchers have conceived of management fashions as ideas and techniques that fail to become firmly rooted because organizations, and the people who work in them, display an ephemeral attachment to them (Abrahamson 1996; Abrahamson and Fairchild 1999; Benders and van Veen 2001; Spell 1999, 2001; Gibson and Tesone 2001). Over the last fifty years these have included ideas such as T-groups, the Managerial Grid, Management by Objectives, Quality-of-Worklife programs, "Excellence," Culture Change, Theory X and Y, Theory Z, Total Quality Management, Quality Circles, Lean Production, Business Process Reengineering (BPR), Knowledge Management, and Six Sigma, among many others.

In a seminal paper on management fashion, Abrahamson (1996) argues that it is "the product of a management-fashion-setting *process* involving particular management fashion setters—organizations and individuals who dedicate themselves to producing and disseminating management knowledge" (1996: 256). He argues that groups of interrelated knowledge entrepreneurs and industries, identified primarily as management consultants, management gurus, business schools, and mass media organizations, are characterized as being in a "race" to sense managers' emergent collective preferences for new ideas and techniques. He terms this group of actors the "fashion-setting community" and argues that they each develop rhetorics which aim to "convince fashion followers that a management technique is both rational and at the forefront of managerial progress" (Abrahamson 1996: 267). Their long-term success is therefore based on the ability to communicate to a broad managerial audience a set of principles in relation to management and organization that involve both a critique of current ways of thinking and a set of prescriptions on how to move towards their conception of the organization (Abrahamson 1996: 267–8; Kieser 1997). In summary, this literature indicates that as members of the management-fashion-setting community, gurus are fundamentally purveyors of management fashion and their speeches and books are the main conduits through which they communicate their ideas to a broad audience.

The very term "management guru" has clear religious connotations. These spill over into discussions and characterizations of their live performances. To date the literature has overwhelmingly tended to view these as quasi-religious events. They are therefore characterized as exercises in persuasive communication where the purpose is to transform the consciousness of the audience to the guru's way of thinking (Clark and Salaman 1996, 1998; Huczynski 2007; Jackson 2001, 2002). This broad picture of management guru events was first expounded in Huczynski's seminal study of management gurus. He wrote that

> it is in his interest to make a convert . . . How can a speaker persuade members of his audience to his way of thinking if they are not already predisposed to it? A realistic aim of the guru's persuasive communication is not that his ideas should necessarily and immediately modify the *actions* of his audience, but that they should alter their *beliefs, attitudes* and *feelings* towards his suggestions.
>
> (Huczynski 2007 [1993]: 245)

To change audience members' commitment to their current thinking about topics and subjects, the guru has to "unhook them from their existing view or beliefs, convert them to his thinking, and then reinforce his ideas so that they are sustained in his absence" (2007: 250). To illustrate how this is achieved, Huczynski adopts Lewin's (1951) three-phase change model to argue that these lectures are broadly characterized by three key interlinked stages. The *unfreezing* phase creates the conditions that are necessary if members of the audience are to be open to changes in their normative world-views. The next stage is the *changing* phase where, through a combination of "push-and-pull factors" (p. 257), the audience's thinking is aligned to that of the guru as they come to appreciate the significance then absorb and accept the ideas being advocated. The final stage—*refreezing*—occurs after the completion of the management guru's performance and involves the gurus seeking to maintain a personal connection with audience members and continuing awareness of their ideas by selling copies of DVDs of their performances, giving away free copies of their books, and offering follow-up consultancy packages, further talks, and free access to their websites, blogs, and email updates.

Huczynski's (2007) description of the unfolding nature of gurus' live performances and the reasons for their potential impact on audience members is detailed and insightful and has consequently been highly influential (see Jackson 2001; ten Bos and Huesinkveld 2007). Indeed, it reflects a largely unquestioned caricature that permeates the great majority of descriptions of these events and so results in a reinforcement of their quasi-religious status. For example, Caulkin (1997: 14) describes Tom Peters' style of lecturing in the following way: "He rants, sweats, stomps up and down and manipulates the emotions of his middle-management audience with the skill of an old-time evangelist." Baur (1994) portrays gurus as "management evangelists" and "corporate hot gospellers" with a talent for phrase-making. Krohe (2004: 34) writes that gurus on the international lecture circuit "Like any successful preacher . . . need to find new sins, new sinners, new paths to salvation to keep their message fresh (and their audiences awake)." Summarizing this broad depiction of management gurus' lecturing style, Greatbatch and Clark note:

> gurus' live lectures are repeatedly portrayed as equivalent to evangelical religious revivalist meetings. They are evangelists who pass among their flock. Their talks are replete with parables about companies and individuals that saw the light and were saved. They are presented as whipping their "congregations" into a state of hysterical compliance with their message by engaging in hellfire preaching.
>
> (Greatbatch and Clark 2005: 21–2)

As they point out, in these, and other characterizations, the gurus' approach and style are seen as identical to that of well-known evangelical preachers such as Billy Graham, Martin Luther King, Jesse Jackson, and, from an earlier period, John Wesley.

Clark and Salaman (1996) have also pursued the religious analogy by arguing that the public presentations of management gurus resemble the performance of a witchdoctor. They point out that the following description of a witchdoctor's work contains some of the same features that the literature on guru performances has highlighted in the previous pages:

The Zande witchdoctor . . . held public séances at which he divined the cause of the misfortunes, including illness, that sufferers brought him. Public séances were rather festive events . . . The performers wore special hats and ornaments and used special tools as whistles and medicines . . . they danced and sang to the accompaniment of lay drums and gongs until they worked themselves into a state of exhaustion. At this point spectators who wished to determine or divine the source of some problem gave gifts ("fees") to the performers. A witchdoctor took a long time to answer these questions, first asking the "patient" a number of questions.

(Freidson 1970: 6)

For Clark and Salaman (1996) this quotation suggests that the witchdoctor performance and the lecturing activities of management gurus are comparable in that they involve some or all of the following: a staged setting supported by a range of theatrical paraphernalia; an emphasis on showmanship; an energetic and passionate style of presentation; direct interaction with audience members; the creation of an intense experience; the revealing of insights that change audience members' ways of thinking.

Clark and Salaman's (1996) work is important because it provides a bridge between the literature on management gurus and celebrities in that Rojek (2001: 53–6) draws a link between shamanism and celebrity. He writes that there are "inescapable parallels with religious worship . . . Celebrities are thought to possess God-like qualities by some fans, while others—experiencing the power of celebrity to arouse deep emotions—recognize the spirit of the shaman" (2001: 53). While we cannot do away with the term "management guru," these latter writers are suggesting that a more appropriate depiction may be as a management witchdoctor or shaman. But, as we have argued in Chapter 2, the problem with such terms is that they focus attention on the individuals and their special abilities rather than the processes which construct and position them as being at the center of this phenomenon. As we stated from the outset, whether we appreciate it or not, celebrity figures of this type are orchestrated co-productions involving a range of cultural intermediaries. We are not denying that management gurus are very capable speakers. If they were not then they would be unable to sustain a large audience following over many years. Nevertheless, while these events rely on the personal appearance of the speaker as their main attraction they are collaboratively produced since they necessarily involve the input of a variety of parties. They are organized and actively promoted by specialist agencies who create posters and mailings, such as that in Figure 3.1, which project these events as speaker centered in that they are portrayed as opportunities to listen to great thinkers and originators of important ideas. These organizations in turn collaborate with other bodies (e.g., universities, chambers of commerce, regional development bodies, and government agencies) in order to generate greater visibility and reach with the potential audience. Frequently they are cross-promoted by the guru's own consultancy. Where this occurs, clients of the consultancy are invited at a special rate and as part of their package get to commune with the guru at a private meal. In addition, the venue uses catering, staging, lighting, and recording contractors in order to enhance the overall experience of delegates. Although these events intentionally celebrate the individuality of gurus, the collaboration between the many parties just identified means that they are elaborate co-productions. From this perspective, management gurus are not solely responsible for their success; rather they are the product of collaborative processes. In this respect, they are best viewed as management fashion celebrities in the sense advanced in Chapter 2.

Seeing them in this way focuses our attention on the processes by which they initially acquire their celebrity status rather than on the apparent manifestations of their activities. It therefore turns our attention from their front-stage activities to their back-stage production. As we argued at the outset of this book, like other business celebrities gurus are not individuals who necessarily achieve their status following broad acknowledgment of, in their case, special and superior communication skills and insights into organizational issues. Would-be gurus come from a number of occupational backgrounds (academia, consultancy, and business) and vary in the level and nature of their accomplishments. Indeed, many gurus appear to rely more on their organizational affiliations to highly respected universities and/or consultancy organizations than specific individual achievements. A common criticism of modern-day celebrity is that many people who appear to have achieved very little, or in some cases nothing, gain celebrity status. As Boorstin (1961: 57) pointed out nearly fifty years ago in a much cited definition, a celebrity is a "human pseudo-event," a person "known for their well-knownness." The point here is that although many people do become celebrities on the basis of a particular achievement (artistic, military, sporting, etc.), this is not a prerequisite. Rather, celebrity is ascribed to people who have acquired a heightened media profile for whatever reason. For Boorstin it is the level of media attention and public awareness this generates that distinguishes the celebrity, rather than any demonstrable achievement which

Figure 3.1 The promotion of management guru events is carefully orchestrated to highlight exclusively the importance of the guru, while keeping all the other producers and promoters of the event behind the curtain.

Source: Reproduced by kind permission of Benchmark for Business

underpins celebrity status. Emphasizing this point, Boorstin writes: "The hero was distinguished by his achievement; the celebrity by his image or trademark. The hero created himself; the celebrity is created by the media. The hero was a big man; the celebrity is a big name" (1961: 61). Gamson's (1994) example of Angelyne exemplifies this point. Her image was displayed on billboards in Los Angeles in the late 1980s. She subsequently appeared in magazines and on television programmes and even in a few films. As Gamson reports, the fact that she and those who supported her denied that she had any particular talent, apart from her appearance and image, leads him to ask the question, "Is celebrity a commodity that can be manufactured through publicity" (1994: 2–4). He concludes that fame can be manufactured and celebrity is fundamentally about getting attention for a particular individual, regardless of their achievements or level of talent. Like Boorstin, he argues that being well known and very visible, in that someone is always in the public eye, is more important than demonstrating any specific gift. One just has to think of the careers of people who either win or participate in reality television programs. Building on this point, Rein, Kotler, and Stoller argue that given the importance of visibility to celebrity, it has now become "an end in itself ":

> So great is the value of visibility that the manufacturing of and marketing of celebrities now reaches into business, sports, entertainment, religion, the arts, politics, academics, medicine, and law. Visibility is what every aspiring hostess wants, what every professional seeks. It is the crucial ingredient that can make lawyer X the most sought after in town, talk show host Y the most popular in her market, and surgeon Z the most highly paid in his city.
>
> (Rein, Kotler, and Stoller 1987: 3)

Drawing on this argument, in what follows we focus on the process by which a management thinker and writer's visibility is elevated to such a point that they become a management fashion celebrity. We will show that their celebrity status is produced by a system that comprises a range of actors and institutions that collaborate to fashion a person's well-knownness. In the process they treat an individual like any commodity or product. As Rojek (2001) has argued, "No celebrity acquires public recognition without the assistance of cultural intermediaries who operate to stage manage celebrity presence in the eyes of the public" (2001: 10). The point here is that management thinkers, like other business celebrities, do not arrive spontaneously and ready-made but are fabricated by a range of different people whose task is to devise the public presentation of the individual and their ideas in such a way that they will have an enhanced visibility and a broad appeal for the intended audience. More specifically in terms of what follows, the combined work of these business culture intermediaries is intended to launch a management writer so that they become quickly attributed as a leading management fashion celebrity by the mass media and in turn the management audience. To show this at work we now turn to examine in detail the process by which best-selling management books become produced.

The production of the management fashion celebrity

In this section we draw on the findings of a study of the production of six best-selling management books (Clark and Greatbatch 2002, 2003). In each case semi-structured interviews were conducted with a range of individuals concerned with the production of each book, namely authors, editors and publishers. We began by contacting the authors, editors, and publishers of each book. Where these individuals mentioned that other personnel had been involved with the production of a book, these people in turn were contacted and where possible interviews conducted. It became apparent that a number of editors and ghost-writers who work freelance had been involved in the production of more than one of these books. We thus spoke to some individuals about the creation of several books.

The guru product

Analysis of the interviews reveals the extent to which best-selling management books are manufactured contrivances that emerge from a creative process in which the form of the presentation of management ideas takes precedence over their actual use value. This is reflected in the fact that the editors and ghost-writers distinguished between these books and other texts aimed at a managerial audience in two ways. First, the ideas and manuscripts that were deemed to have blockbuster potential were regarded as star-based products; that is, as vehicles for promoting the visibility of the authors and their brand (Tom Peters is the undisputed master of this practice (see Figure 3.2)). As one editor stated, "The author is all-important. What we want is to

Figure 3.2 Author Tom Peters sits among stacks of his new books waiting to be autographed at his home in Tinmouth, VT, on August 31, 1999.

Source: Photographer: Toby Talbott. Reproduced with permission from the Associated Press.

build a brand so that the author has instant recognition. This will help when we come to publish their future books and develop synergistic lines." Another editor explained that these books were star vehicles in the following terms:

> [w]hen you publish these books you have to work on the assumption that most people who buy it won't read it. It needs to be seductive for reasons other than content. The package is the total package, the book and the person . . . Packaging the author is as important as packaging the book. We promote the person as much as the book . . . What you are selling is an attachment to a particular person and their brand or ideas. Our job is either to create this or to develop it further.

Similarly another editor stated: "People don't buy these books if they don't know the author. Part of our task is to help create awareness of the author so that they become known and by association their ideas are talked about."

These quotations underpin a number of key points. First, the success of these books is intimately tied up with the extent to which the author can become well known and visible. Remaining low key or anonymous will harm sales. The book is therefore as much a vehicle for promoting an individual as the ideas it contains. There is a sense from the interviewees and quotations above that there is often a greater stress on the individual and their personality than the merits of the actual ideas contained in the book. This puts a premium on building the brand and well-knownness of the individual so that they become a "big name." As a consequence, their name and ideas become publicly mixed in a way that is difficult to disentangle. Tom Peters is forever linked with "excellence," Peter Senge with the "learning organizations," and Michael Hammer with "reengineering." Editors and publishers are therefore less concerned with identifying and nurturing truly innovative management ideas than building a small stable of star authors.

Second, from the outset it is designed as part of a broader package of related products that will all feature the author. The brand and author's visibility will be leveraged into different areas of activity. As one publisher/editor explained, "the book is just one part of a line of products. These may include seminars, lectures, audio tapes, video-based training packages." In this respect the logic of the "star system" in Hollywood also operates in the market for guru products. According to this logic, the star/guru functions as an anchor that coordinates the promotion of a number of ancillary products across a range of different platforms. Developing a strong brand for an author and would-be guru is seen as a way of almost guaranteeing purchases from different elements of their product range. In this way celebrity gurus feed a number of "satellite" or related industries that in turn further build and sustain gurus' attention-getting power and celebrity status. Similarly, when leading film stars promote their latest movie they not only project their films to a broad potential audience but by giving interviews and attending premières they support a range of related activities, from celebrity magazines and newspapers to television shows and blogs. Such a range of communication outlets which feature them prominently ensures that the potential audience has a number of methods through which they and their film can be encountered. They become brands that transcend any particular film and are difficult to avoid. Although on a smaller scale, one can always attend a guru lecture, a training course, listen to a CD, or watch a DVD of a recorded lecture, or visit their website and read their blog. What this suggests is that the value of an idea is increasingly less about its inherent merits and organizational benefits and more about its ability to be packaged into a plethora of related products that build and sustain awareness of the guru. However, as we shall argue later, there is a hierarchy within this assortment of related products in that the book is clearly viewed as the foundation for subsequent products.

A further issue arising from the previous point is that editors do not regard potential gurus as a fixed product that is ready to sell. In this respect, gurus' ideas are not viewed as immutable objects in which the purity of the authors' original concept is sacrosanct. Rather these are books that require shaping prior to publication, if they are to be made attractive to the intended audience. The initial idea is generally viewed as no more than raw material that has to be further developed and molded before it can be published as a book. Editors, therefore, are not seeking fully formed books that can be published with minimal copy-editing, but rather the glimmer of an idea that they believe can be shaped and packaged to appeal to a management audience, and to promote the author and their brand. As one editor noted:

> There is no general requirement in terms of the amount of detail we expect from the outset. We take on some books with detailed synopses of each chapter and the first chapter written. Other books start off as a one-page summary of a series of ideas. What I am looking for is something that will appeal to an audience no matter how detailed.

Making a similar point, when referring to a particularly successful book, another editor stated: "I liked the concept. We didn't have much to go on initially, just some loose descriptions of the chapters. I knew if we pitched the content in the right way it would do well."

These quotations and discussion also demonstrate that the focus of transformational processes in the guru industry, from the viewpoint of editors, is the book and the presentation and structure of the ideas. Unlike the Hollywood celebrity system it does not appear to involve considerable personal transformation. Writing about the process by which people are transformed into celebrities, Rein, Kotler, and Stoller (1987) state, "*The idea is to select or invent a unique, or at least distinct, combination of factors that will distinguish one aspirant from the rest*" (1987: 198, italics in the original). This can involve different levels of personal transformation, including a change of identity with the use of a stage name, changes in appearance, whether the result of natural or physically assisted processes, even changes in character and personality (projected or real). On occasion the outcome can be such that what is viewed as a natural quality can in fact be a manufactured ornamentation. The processes of transformation are not always clear even though popular celebrity magazines are full of stories that follow in minute detail individual celebrity transformations. Furthermore, one just has to observe the changes made to contestants participating in television talent shows from the auditions to the televised knock-out stage of the contest to see the outcome of some of these processes. For gurus, personal changes often involve moving from wearing glasses to contact lenses, and changes in hairstyle and clothing. These are all aimed at giving the guru a more professional business look and at the same time improving their ability to present their ideas to live audiences. Research shows that not being able to see a speaker's eyes and teeth can reduce their ability to obtain an appropriate audience response (Greatbatch and Clark 2005).

Having established that the editors are primarily concerned not with the utility of management books but rather with their potential as star vehicles which can be used to build and promote an author's brand, we now turn to discuss how this shapes the writing and editing process prior to publication.

Collaboration

Best-selling management books, like many cultural and consumer products, "do not spring forth full blown but are made somewhere by somebody" (Peterson 1979: 152). The displayed character of a potentially best-selling management book at the point of publication is the result of active collaboration at earlier stages between the originator(s) and a range of support personnel rather than being the work of a single person (i.e., the author). In this sense these management books are collective social products that depend for their character on reciprocal collaboration between a network of support personnel (Clark and Greatbatch 2002, 2003). Thus, the milieu within which they are produced shapes the form and content of the ideas prior to their presentation to the target audience.

Building on this point Becker (1974) has observed that cultural products require a range of people to interact with the artist if they are to be presented to the intended audience. Although we may associate them with a particular person at the point when they are consumed, their production takes place via the interaction of a variety of different interested parties, much like the celebrification process we described in Chapter 2. To illustrate this point he uses the example of a symphony orchestra giving a concert. For this to take place,

> instruments must have been invented, manufactured and maintained, a notation must have been devised and music composed using that notation,

people must have learned to play the notated notes on the instruments, times and places for rehearsal must have been provided, ads for the concert must have been placed, publicity arranged and tickets sold, and an audience capable of listening to and in some way understanding and responding to the performance must have been recruited.

(Becker 1974: 767)

Becker's point is that no individual artist has the breadth of skill and level of talent that they can do everything. In the case of a piece of music they cannot compose the music as well as make all the instruments required for its performance, perform all the instruments, book the venue, publicize the event, as well as stand in as the audience. Musicians need help from others (e.g., record companies, producers, arrangers, and publicists). Similarly, painters often need some form of sponsorship and support from collectors and gallery owners. Becker's key point is that every artistic act is inherently and necessarily collaborative. He writes, "Whatever the artist, so defined, does not do himself must be done by someone else . . . Wherever he depends on others, a co-operative link exists" (1974: 769). Building on this key observation, any analysis of a cultural product must therefore focus on the broader community who help in creating and sustaining the career of an individual artist. Becker (1982: 34) has termed this network of support personnel an "art world" which he defines specifically as "all people whose activities are necessary to the production of the characteristic works which that world, and perhaps others as well, define as art." Usually, their identity is hidden or acknowledged only in passing.

Given that these books are collaborative co-productions, a key role of the editor is to carefully combine and manage the talents of authors and other support personnel in such a way that a book has the best chance of success when released into the marketplace. On some occasions the team may be limited to the author and editor. At other times it may include additional support personnel such as ghost-writers. As the following quotations illustrate the decision with respect to the composition of a team relates to the editor's evaluation of a number of factors:

It's funny because it was originally intended as a collaborative process but [named person] got over-committed and I found myself having to do it alone. The editor at [the publisher] put me in touch with someone who became my unacknowledged co-author. I think they felt that I still needed some kind of collaboration.

> I think that we were an unknown quantity . . . I was busy and we kept missing deadlines and the project looked like stalling. Our editor suggested that we work with someone to give the book broader appeal. He was quite inspirational. He liked what we were doing. Found lots of "wows" in our research. He gave us encouragement and got us back on track.

These different quotations show that collaborators are chosen in response to some particular circumstances in terms of the production of each book. In one instance a co-author withdrew from the project; in the other several authors had consistently missed deadlines and the editor recognized that they needed to find a way to reinvigorate the writing process. The encouragement from the ghost-writer clearly worked in this instance. As the following editor/author describes, in addition to these factors they also used their evaluation of the success or failure of books on which they had worked previously, competing books in the marketplace, and their understanding of the position of an idea in terms of the cycle of its popular appeal.

> I watched vision and vision statements become a fad in the mid eighties and we never published anything on that. We missed the fashion curve on that one . . . I noticed that conferences on this topic were increasing. I also thought, my hunch was, my intuition was that this topic was becoming a fad and I felt if we were going to publish a book on the subject we should publish it at the beginning of the fad.

In this case the editor wanted to publish a book on an emerging topic. In order to publish before potentially competitive titles emerged, the author worked with a ghost writer.

Despite these factors, the key issue that all the editors emphasized was their evaluation of the author's competence as a writer. One editor/ghost-writer justified both ghost-writing and extensive editorial input during the writing process in the following terms:

> Many "authors" can't or won't write. But they may be gifted as thinkers, presenters, synthesizers, commentators, speakers, or entertainers . . . We often assume that if a person is a talented speaker, presenter, motivator, mentor, professor, consultant, trainer, or professional that he or she must also be capable of writing a wonderful book. Wrong. I often use a track and field metaphor. If a person is world class at the

400 meter hurdles, does that mean the same person should also be world class at the 100 meter sprint, the mile, the high jump, or the marathon?

This comment relates to the point made earlier in the chapter that the editors seek to build brands that can then be leveraged into a number of media. In pursuing this strategy an author does not necessarily have to be judged by editors/ghost-writers to be a competent or potential writer of a best-selling management book. As we shall discuss later in the chapter, there are occasions when a book is completely fabricated. As one editor/publisher explained, "One of our strategies is to take people who are popular speakers and with a good profile and to present them with an idea . . . We do the concept development and writing and they get a book to push." The point here is that not every would-be guru needs to demonstrate that they are an accomplished wordsmith. If they are seen to be an excellent live presenter but a poor writer the insinuation is that this can be overcome with the aid of strong editorial input or the employment of a ghost-writer. In view of this we now turn to examine the role of editors and ghost-writers in more detail.

Conventions

Central to editors' and ghost-writers' conceptions of popular management writing is a set of textual conventions that pervade best-selling management books. Becker (1974: 770–1) notes that for a work of art, conventions underpin who will cooperate, how they will work together, and the form of the work that is the focus of the joint endeavor. It is these conventions that are at the heart of the celebrification of these books, since they package the ideas in such a way that the published book is likely to be visible, to appeal to the intended audience, and to promote the author's brand. The conventions derive from, and are justified by reference to, a shared conception of those who purchase best-selling management books. Based on the information sources referred to above, editors/ghost-writers view managers as being extremely busy with a focus on the tangible and immediate and a tendency towards superficiality and short attention spans. An editor reminded one of the gurus in our study that he was

> writing for managers who are relatively intelligent and can take ideas to work with them, and who are very busy. And a key market for my books was people who take four or five hour flights. When I think of my readers

now, I think that on the whole managers read on airplanes, or they take my books on holiday which I find a compliment.

Another of the gurus was advised by his editor to "write clearly and have your readers in mind. It's got to be easily digestible and memorable. Managers are busy people and do not want to wade through lots of waffle." Making a similar point an editor described their approach to these books as: "stripping the ideas to their essence and making sure that the reader is not diverted into irrelevant material. These books need to communicate directly or they will bore the reader."

In the light of this conception of the intended audience for these management books, editors/ghost-writers aim to present the ideas in accessible forms that have two characteristics. The first is that they are easy to read and remember. This requires that the main elements of the ideas be reduced and simplified into pithy lists, acronyms, concepts, mnemonics, metaphors, and stories that are immediately graspable, understood, and assimilated. One editor described their approach to conveying ideas in these books as: "making the core proposition crystal clear. There is no room for ambiguity. From the outset the central themes have to be grouped into a model, framework or list of principles. You want the readers to know what an idea stands for." In a similar vein a guru reflecting on the process by which their first best-selling book was written stated:

> Writing the book in this way with [the editor] was a wonderfully reflective process and it led to a way of organizing the ideas that I had not planned at the outset. The grouping of the ideas into a number of general principles came with the book writing. So the book writing tied together a number of loose-ends in my thinking and in the process made them more accessible.

Second, the editors/ghost-writers use forms that emphasize and demonstrate the practical relevance of the gurus' ideas. They need to be made vivid and concrete for the audience. Often this involves relating stories of how the gurus' ideas have been successfully implemented in many organizations. Thus, the gurus were exhorted to include examples of their principles being put into practice in order to persuade readers that their analysis and solutions were not only relevant but also the most appropriate. As one guru was told, "you gotta show them that it really works. Who's going to buy into something that's never been tried?" Another was given the advice that "in telling stories you have to show that the idea behind the story is backed up by rigorous research but also company practice. So, you have to tell stories about real managers facing real problems in real organizations. Doing this makes the idea more real to the reader."

This last quotation indicates that for some editors the examples are there to show the readers that the gurus' ideas work in practice. Similarly, a ghost-writer/editor stated: "My 'litmus test' is have the concepts of the author ever been applied in a real company with favorable results? Do they make a real difference even at an individual personal level?" The assumption underlying these statements is that if a reader can see that organizations have implemented the changes advocated by the author then it is also possible for the reader and/or their organization to achieve the same benefits by adopting the author's ideas. These benefits are therefore viewed as transferable. However, comments from another guru indicate that these examples can also serve an alternative function in that they may help to legitimize their vision. This is achieved, in part, by carefully selecting organizations that are household names and therefore well-known to the readers of these books, possibly even admired by them. As this guru stated, "the companies chosen had to be recognizable to large numbers of people otherwise they will think so what. But if X, Y, or Z did this then it must really be important." As another guru said:

> I had been working with a number of well-known organizations for many years. I knew the ideas worked. The point of the book was to share their experiences and success with a wider audience so that we could form a critical mass as more organizations became aware of and sought to implement the ideas. One area where [the editor] was really helpful was in getting me to illustrate the ideas with some well-chosen examples.

Again what was important was to present the ideas in such a way that the readers felt that they too could implement what the guru was advocating.

In sum, editors/ghost-writers have a significant, if largely unseen, impact on the fashioning of management ideas in book form. They shape and package ideas in line with conventions that are associated with best-selling management books. These findings support earlier work by Kieser (1997), Furusten (1999), and Røvik (2002), who each sought to identify the ingredients of best-selling management books. Their work has similarly stressed the importance of the following: (1) a single concept or model condensed into an easy-to-remember/"catchy" acronym; (2) lists, metaphors, stories, and short sentences with simple language to enhance readability; (3) the use of well-known exemplar companies to both legitimize the ideas and stress their practical and universal benefits; (4) a mix of simplicity and ambiguity; and (5) timing. The latter factor is particularly important. As Kieser (1997: 61) notes, "all these ingredients are useless if the timing is not perfect. The book must hit the 'nerve of today's managers.' "

Interviews with editors/ghost-writers and gurus revealed the extent to which management ideas are mediated through these conventions. This raises important questions concerning the extent to which the gurus' original/existing ideas are reconfigured and changed as editors and ghost-writers render them accessible to the intended managerial audience. It is clear that these conventions are not neutral conduits that simply amplify and enhance the authors' original ideas. As the following quotations indicate, several of the gurus remarked that the form of their ideas changed substantially during the writing/editing process:

> I think my first draft was all over the place. It was probably double the length of the final manuscript. I probably produced about five or six complete drafts. Each one would go to [the editor] and they would write back with loads of comments and suggestions. I tell you, if you saw that first draft you wouldn't recognize the published book.

> The hardest thing when writing the book was that I had written all these darn academic papers all my life. I had never written a book. I was very fortunate in that I had a wonderful editor who was a great consultant. He really helped to deconstruct my writing style. He would write samples of what he thought would work for the audience, which I never liked and so rewrote them. He also told me to bring my personal speaking voice in to my writing which was hard. It was a real learning process which did produce a different kind of book. But I was pleased with that.

> I had written other things before but not a book so as I wrote a draft I would send it to [the editor]. They would send me pages of comments and we would talk on the telephone. This happened many times and through this process the ideas became clearer and the key concepts emerged.

It is clear from the comments that the editing process for a number of the gurus actively shaped and modified their initial ideas so that what was presented to the target audience was qualitatively different from the draft manuscript or book outline that entered the publishing system. Although in the first two cases they felt that the finished book was better for this intervention, it was nevertheless changed from what they had originally envisaged. None of the gurus whose books had been subject to extensive editorial input viewed this in negative terms. Rather they portrayed themselves as naïve first-time authors who did not have the necessary skills to write a book (see Clark and Greatbatch 2002). In this respect they concur with the views of the ghost-writer who earlier argued that many authors are skilled public orators but poor writers. They thus recognize that their skills are limited in some areas and require appropriate assistance to make up for this deficiency.

While the character of these books often changed during the editorial process some changed more than others, depending on the level of author input and control over the writing process. However, one publisher explained that in a small number of cases their books were complete inventions from the outset in that they admitted to first coming up with an idea and then pitching it to an established author/speaker. They then employed someone to write the book while the guru lent their name to it. In each case this phenomenon related to a guru's second, third, fourth book, and so on. These manufactured books, which usually involve the refashioning and development of a guru's existing ideas, are important to both gurus and editors. Every two or three years gurus need a new book to fuel the demand for their services on the corporate lecture circuit (Farnham 1996). Similarly, the editors are under pressure to extend the life of the guru's brand in order to maximize the publishers' revenues from their established authors. One UK publisher gave the following example of a manufactured book:

> [Guru's name] had written *Heart* [this is a pseudonym] and we thought of the idea of *More Heart* [also a pseudonym]. We proposed this to him. He does not receive any money. We pay the ghost-writer. But it extends [guru's name] mini-brand and is something else he can promote on the conference circuit. Manufacturing books is very very easy for authors to be involved in . . . We get a big name, they get a new book for little effort. We all benefit. These people don't want to publish for money. What they want is the prestige of having a book in print.

Although by no means all gurus are involved in the manufacture of books, this phenomenon reflects the relative status of books and other media used to disseminate management ideas. As we have indicated, the management gurus included in the present study do not restrict their communication activities to books alone, but they also speak on the international lecture circuit, make DVD and audio programs, produce CDs, and establish Internet sites. It could be argued that these other media are just as able, if not better in certain circumstances, at conveying their ideas in an easily apprehendable and succinct manner. However, they would appear not to have displaced the premier status of the book. The book was generally viewed as a necessary prerequisite for access to the other media.

This suggests that a best-selling book represents an entry ticket into the broad range of media through which popular management ideas can be communicated. Thus, while some of the gurus included in the present study have reduced the number of live presentations they give a year and have withdrawn from making audio and video programs, not one has stopped writing books. They all see it as a fundamental way of communicating their ideas. Indeed, several gurus consider their long-term popularity to be linked to their ability to continue to publish books. For example, one guru stated: "My books are part of my public identity. When people introduce you, you come over as having something to say if they can say 'and here is so and so author of such and such a book.'" However, their increasing commitment to the international speaking circuit or consulting work that arises from their celebrity status means that they may not have either the time or the inclination to develop a further set of novel ideas for follow-up books. This is where the manufacturing of books plays a crucial role in their continuing status as management gurus.

So important are best-selling books to launching a guru and their ideas that some authors may have sought to artificially inflate their sales figures and in the process influence the best-seller lists. For example, in 1995, *BusinessWeek* exposed an intricate scheme that manipulated the sales of Treacy and Wiersema's *The Discipline of Market Leaders* (1995) to guarantee that it entered the *New York Times* best-seller list. Employees of CSC Index, which had been the birthplace for Hammer and Champy's *Reengineering the Corporation* (1993) and where the two authors worked, appeared to have used around $250,000 to purchase over 10,000 copies of the book. *BusinessWeek* further claimed that CSC Index bought an additional 30,000 to 40,000 copies as "corporate purchases" through carefully targeted bookshops with the aim of improving the book's position on the *New York Times* best-seller list. The article suggests that by splitting purchases across a large number of bookshops in the USA they were not picked up as bulk "corporate purchases" and so would be included in any sales figures and thereby impact positively on the book's position in the best-seller list.

Management fashion celebrities and images of heroic managers

This chapter has shown that management fashion celebrities are produced through a range of background collaborative processes. As we emphasized in Chapter 2, it is essential that would-be celebrities achieve what we have called traction. To do this they need to be perceived as attractive by a range of agents and interested parties at different stages in the celebrification process. Thus, before they can be the acclaimed author of a best-selling book and successful international speaker with a range of CDs and DVDs they have to demonstrate potential to key gatekeepers; in this case editors and publishers. It is these individuals and organizations that can either block or facilitate their widespread exposure to the target audience as well as traction across different media since these are founded on the publication of a best-selling book. Without the active assistance of these support personnel and organizations, these management thinkers and writers would not achieve the level of visibility necessary for celebrity status.

A celebrity management thinker is therefore not a solo performer with rare abilities and insight. They may be talented, but their celebrity status is conferred upon them as a result of the joint endeavors of all those people who cooperate in the creation, fashioning, and projection of their ideas to the target audience. Without this network of collaborative relationships, the people featured in the chapter would remain "would be" management fashion celebrities. This suggests that the success of a guru is, in large part, determined by the composition of their support network. Different combinations and networks may increase or decrease the chances of someone becoming a management fashion celebrity.

With respect to the latter part of the chapter, it is clear that cooperation among the actors within the network is based upon generalized beliefs, or conventions, of what makes a legitimate and successful management book. As we have indicated, one of the main functions of the system is to impart these conventions to nascent gurus in order to increase the likelihood of their book becoming a best-seller and the individual move to celebrity status. This is not to suggest that these conventions are immutable. They evolve and transform in response to shifts in the broader business environment and consumer preferences with the consequence that what is deemed an appropriate management book also changes. For example, as we discuss in Chapter 5, the string of corporate scandals in America that followed the collapse of Enron and the fall of countless celebrity bosses challenged not simply the celebratory tone of the guru best-seller genre, but also its legitimacy. This arises from the key position of popular management books within the institutional fabric that supported the rise of the celebrity CEO. As Khurana (2002a) has argued, the media, broadly defined, "focus not on the complexities of organizations or on rapid changes in the business environment, but rather on the actors involved. This approach personifies the corporation, making much of winners and losers, of who is up and who is down, of who is a good CEO and who is not. The press has thereby turned CEO's . . . into a new category of American celebrity" (2002a: 74). This resonates with Clark and Salaman's argument that popular management theory is successful not because it "solves" managers' problems but because it constitutes the role itself. These books define the management role by offering "a conception of management itself in virtuous, heroic, high status terms" (1998: 157).

From this point of view, guru best-sellers generate their appeal by articulating the qualities necessary for successful implementation of the management role. As we show in this chapter, those involved in the production of these books mold the nature and presentation of the ideas for a specific audience—managers. In doing so these books are presented in such a way that they reinforce why managers are important, why they matter, and why their skills are critical. However, the wave of corporate scandals in the past few years has led to the questioning of the very image that these books seek to project. Continuing to laud the exploits of hero managers is no longer deemed appropriate. Indeed, while these books continue to sell it is clear that their shine has begun to fade. Consequently, more cynical books, such as Scott Adams's subversive Dilbert cartoons, have topped the management best-seller lists (London 2003; *The Economist* 2002).

As this chapter has made clear, the management guru phenomenon is all about the creation of images—images of gurus as the authors of their own books and the generators of their own ideas and insights, and images of the consumers of guru products as more effective and even more heroic managers because of their familiarity with the gurus and their ideas. In the next chapter we continue this discussion of images with respect to another kind of business celebrity—the hero manager or celebrity CEO. Towards this end, we draw on our previous research on the visual representation of prominent CEOs and business leaders to explore the centrality of photographs and other images to the construction of business celebrity. We point out that celebrity is just as much about face recognition as it is about name recognition or attribution in printed texts. And the centrality of visual images to the processes of celebrity production and reproduction reinforces the approach we have developed in this chapter. That is, like celebrities themselves, visual representations and images of celebrities function as forms of social interaction, dialogue, and debate over what it means to be a person in a society dominated by large business institutions.

4 The many faces of business celebrity

If you type the words "Bill Gates" in quotation marks into an image search engine on the Internet, here is a small sampling of the images you will find:

Bill Gates on the cover of *Time Magazine*. Bill Gates with Bono. Bill Gates with Steve Jobs. Bill Gates with the president. Bill Gates with the queen. Bill Gates with the Hooters girls. Bill Gates with an African baby. Bill Gates with a computer. Bill Gates on a boat. Bill Gates near a boat. Bill Gates in a bathtub. Bill Gates in front of Congress. Bill Gates at a desk. Bill Gates on a desk. Bill Gates at a podium. Bill Gates at Comdex. Bill Gates at Davos. Bill Gates at Microsoft headquarters. Bill Gates as a geek with impossibly large glasses. Bill Gates as a nice guy in a casual sweater. Bill Gates as a great philanthropist. Bill Gates as a skinny college dropout. Bill Gates as a world leader. Bill Gates as a common criminal. Bill Gates as Chairman Mao. Bill Gates as George Washington crossing the Delaware [see Figure 4.1]. Bill Gates as a brown-shirted Nazi leading a horde of jack-booted storm troopers. Meet Bill Gates. Punch Bill Gates. Throw a pie at Bill Gates. Throw tomatoes and eggs at Bill Gates. Kill Bill Gates [these images play on the title and posters for the Quentin Tarantino film, *Kill Bill*]. Hit Bill Gates' head around like a hockey puck.

The number of photographs, cartoons, and other visual representations of Bill Gates available out there is simply staggering. They range from candid snapshots to official portraits, from glossy magazine covers to digitally altered images and cartoons on personal blogs. On the day we wrote this sentence (March 6, 2008), a Google search coughed up 1,400,000 such images of the Microsoft founder and formerly richest man in the world (Figure 4.2). That is a huge number, considering that Gates does not exactly have the good looks of a Brad Pitt (who got only 1,280,000 hits on the same day) or a George

Figure 4.1 "Bill Gates Crossing the Delaware." A digitally altered version of the famous 1851 painting by Emanuel Leutze (Sroka 2007).

Source: Reproduced with the generous permission of Daniel Sroka
(http://www.danielsroka.com)

Clooney (869,000). Granted, as a tool for gauging celebrity, the Google image search function lacks scientific rigor. The image count changes slightly from day to day. It repeats some images, misses others, and churns out many that don't depict Bill Gates at all. This is because a search engine like Google cannot really see image content. It looks instead for occurrences of the search term near an image, in a caption, or in a link to that image from somewhere else. But since these caveats also apply to image searches for Brad Pitt, George Clooney, or any other celebrity, the results are still instructive in a comparative sense.

We therefore performed the same search using the names at the top of the *Forbes* magazine "Celebrity 100" list from 2007, which takes a (slightly) more scientific approach than just punching names into Google. "To generate the list," the magazine explains, "Forbes analyzes celebrity earnings, plus media metrics like Google hits, press mentions as compiled by Lexis/Nexis, TV/radio mentions from Factiva and the number of times an A-lister appears on the cover of 32 major consumer magazines" (Goldman *et al.* 2007). When the magazine published this list in June 2007, Oprah Winfrey enjoyed the number-one position. But her name renders only 322,000 images in our Google image survey. Of the top twenty celebrities listed by *Forbes*, in fact, only Johnny Depp and Madonna get more Google image hits than Gates, with

Figure 4.2 Microsoft Windows screen capture of a Google image search performed
on June 18, 2008.

1,630,000 and 6,310,000 respectively. In order to maintain some semblance
of scientific due diligence, we have to throw out that last result as unreliable,
because it clearly includes millions of images of other Madonnas. We had the
same problem with Gates' fellow *Time* Person of the Year, Bono, of the
blockbuster rock band U2 (Figure 4.3). His ambiguously brief moniker
generates 1,990,000 hits, but also unearths too many images that have nothing
to do with the celebrity rock star/activist himself, including many of the late
pop star and US congressman Sonny Bono.

We found only three other celebrities who generated more Google image
hits than Bill Gates, and none of them even makes the *Forbes* ranking these
days—Britney Spears with 3,020,000, Paris Hilton with 2,480,000, and
Michael Jackson with 2,200,000. The only other business figure near the top
of the *Forbes* list—Donald Trump at number nineteen—appears in a mere
184,000 images. Among business figures more generally, the only one who
comes anywhere close to Gates is his erstwhile rival, Steve Jobs, with 984,000
images. So if a Google image search of the Internet is any indicator, Bill Gates
may just be the fifth most visible person in the world—certainly among the
top ten—which attests to his status as a major celebrity.

Figure 4.3 Celebrity cross-fertilization: Bono and Bill and Melinda Gates on the *Time* "Persons of the Year" cover, December 25, 2006.

Source: Photographer: Gregory Heisler. Reproduced with permission from Time Inc.

Interestingly enough, *Forbes* does not even count Gates as a celebrity, placing him instead on a separate list of top billionaires. But there is more than just a fascination with extreme wealth driving the vigorous market for pictures of Bill Gates. With $62 billion in his pocket, Warren Buffett is the wealthiest person in the world as we write this sentence, but he generates only 57,900 images, less than 4 percent as many as Gates. The second wealthiest person, Mexican telecom mogul Carlos Slim Helú, is next to invisible by comparison, with only 19,500 hits. According to our informal image survey, then, Bill Gates is a much bigger celebrity than any of his super-wealthy peers, bigger than most of the people on the *Forbes* Celebrity 100, and hands down the most visible business celebrity in the world.

Our goal in conducting this brief exercise is not to compete with *Forbes* for a piece of the celebrity-ranking game, but rather to point out that the phenomenon of celebrity depends crucially on the production and circulation of photographs, portraits, and other kinds of visual representation. Business celebrity is not just about the attribution of successful skills and character-istics to certain celebrated individuals via newspapers, magazines, and other forms of print media. It is also about the way those individuals *look*, and about the supposed thrill of looking at them—here, there, with so-and-so, at a party, in handcuffs, behind bars. Celebrity is about familiarity, recognition, visibility, and voyeurism. Photographs help turn business figures into celebrities by portraying them like other celebrities, and often by photographing them alongside other celebrities, in ways that promote the kind of abstract desire discussed in the previous chapter. In this sense celebrity is "scopophilic," to borrow a term from Freudian psychology by way of film theory (Mulvey 1975). That is, it depends on the promotion of an obsession with gazing at the object of our desires. This element of riveted fascination derives in large part from the manner in which photographs provide a sense of direct or even intimate contact with business celebrities. In this regard photographs of busi-ness celebrities perform some of the same functions as the live appearances of management gurus that we discuss in Chapter 5, and, indeed, many photo-graphs of business celebrities capture them as they appear in live events.

Rein, Kotler, and Stoller argue that visibility is the driving principle of the celebrity industries, and that it is intrinsic to the meaning of celebrity itself. "High visibility has become a valuable commodity all by itself," they point out. "It is an entity that stands alone, independent of accomplishment, sacrifice, or heroics" (1987: 14). As mentioned in the previous chapter, these authors define a celebrity as "a person whose name has attention-getting, interest-riveting, and profit-generating value" (1987: 15). But their emphasis on the *name* of the celebrity points towards the way that they use the term "visibility" to refer to media exposure in a general and not a specifically visual sense. We have noted elsewhere that many scholars are quick to employ visual metaphors like "visibility," especially the term "image" itself, to point towards decidedly non-visual things like reputations, mental impressions, or public opinions. If we want to talk about *actual* visibility, then we need to define celebrities as "people whose *faces* have attention-getting, interest-riveting, and profit-generating value."

In this chapter we therefore highlight the vital importance of the face and the centrality of actual visual images to the phenomenon of business celebrity. The problem with raising this issue is that, at first glance, photographs and portraits tend to contribute to the idea that celebrity is primarily a matter of certain notable individuals and their distinctive characteristics. This is precisely why visual images are so important to the construction of celebrity itself in the first place. But our own tight focus on the faces of business celebrity need not reinforce this ideological tendency. Taking a close look at images, portraits, and photographs will not lead us away from our argument that celebrity is a form of industrial process and social interaction. To the contrary, a careful consideration of the visual aspects of celebrity production and reproduction reinforces our main point. Like business celebrities themselves, visual representations of business celebrities function as forms of social interaction and as sites where different visions of celebrity meet, interact, and come into open conflict.

As we discuss below, scholars of organization and leadership have paid little attention to visual representations of business celebrities. They have spent a lot of time talking about images and perceptions of organizations and leaders, but they have defined these in primarily verbal, abstract, and meta-phorical terms as something akin to "the picture in our heads." In order to refocus our attention on visual images of business celebrity, we therefore draw on our own previous research to emphasize the importance of portraits of celebrity CEOs and other top executives to the establishment of corporate authenticity, and we summarize our argument concerning what we have called the CEO authenticity paradox. We have used this term to describe the manner in which visual images of high-profile CEOs and other business celebrities both construct and deconstruct authenticity at the same time. The approach we have developed to business celebrity in this book can help to explain why this is the case.

As opposed to the picture in our heads, the many pictures before our eyes are concrete, embedded, multivalent, and open to interpretation. A closer look at these pictures helps to bring into focus the construction of multiple, often conflicting images of the same business celebrity (Bill Gates, for example), the manner in which even individual images invite multiple perspectives and conflicting interpretations, and the involvement of multiple actors and interests in relational processes of image production, dissemination, and interpretation. Images and portraits of CEOs and business celebrities are paradoxical, then, because they function as repositories for multiple, even conflicting perspectives on what authenticity is and whether or not Bill Gates or some other business leader has it. In the last section of this chapter, we summarize the interpretive approach we have developed for approaching visual images of business leadership as sites of interaction, debate, and conflict, and we turn our gaze back to the visual representation of Bill Gates to exemplify how this approach works.

Image research in organization and leadership studies

Visual images flood the landscape of contemporary western society via ever proliferating media channels. The primary language of advertising is visual, as are many products on offer in what has been termed the experience economy (Pine and Gilmore 1999). Pictures have the power not only to move products, but also to shape news and alter political debates, as exemplified by media coverage of the Abu Ghraib prison scandal and the recent wave of protests over cartoons depicting the Prophet Mohammed (Sontag 2004; Arnold *et al.* 2006). At the individual level photographs reaffirm and certify who we are— in family photo albums or passports—to the point where the very notion of identity has become "inconceivable without photography" (Schroeder 2002: 14).

Most of the visual images that saturate contemporary everyday experience are produced and disseminated by commercial organizations. And many of these images seek to convey a visual impression of commercial organizations themselves, or their leaders. Glance at almost any newspaper, business magazine, or corporate annual report and at least one top executive will glance back. Photographs and portraits of well-known or would-be business celebrities have become the ubiquitous media wallpaper of corporate capitalism. CEOs portraits, like the top executives they depict, come in several familiar shapes and sizes—from the elaborately staged publicity stills of businessman heroes (and a few heroines) that dominate annual reports, company websites, and glossy business magazines, to the less flattering, candid photos of indicted

CEOs in handcuffs that punctuate headlines about corporate scandal; from the grip-and-grin snapshots that litter newsletters and press releases, to the idiosyncratic photographic portraits produced by recognized artists that sometimes hang in museums and galleries. Each of these kinds of photograph employs its own visual code and raises its own set of representational, organizational, and ideological issues, although these may overlap or even collide in any given photograph.

Organization and leadership studies have not developed a capacity fully to understand the production or dissemination of such images, nor the central role they play in shaping perceptions of both organizations and leaders. This is rather ironic, given the fact that scholars in these fields have spent so much time talking about image in an extensive amount of research on organizational image, professional image, and leadership images. The problem is that almost all this otherwise valuable research uses words such as "picture," "snapshot," "visibility," and "image" in a metaphorical sense to refer to abstract conceptions or collectively shared mental constructs, and not to concrete visual representations. The majority of such studies define image as a cognitive construct or projection of a collection of attributes or characteristics attached to an individual (e.g., self-image or persona), to a group or class of individuals (e.g., professional image), or to an organization (e.g., organizational or corporate image) (Hatch and Schultz 1997; Ibarra 1999; Gioia *et al.* 2000). Often scholars render the concept even more abstract by stressing aggregate perceptions expressed as a collective whole (e.g., public image; Berg 1985); by stressing the formative influence of news organizations and the commercial press (e.g., media image and refracted image; Chen and Meindl 1991); by stressing individual and organizational attempts to influence those aggregate perceptions (projected image; Bernstein 1984); by stressing what certain individuals or groups think that others perceive (e.g., construed external image; Dutton and Dukerich 1991); or by stressing what certain individuals or groups would like others to perceive (in their minds) in the future (e.g., desired future image; Gioia and Thomas 1996).

The research on image in organization studies has an intellectual history that helps to explain the origins of this preoccupation with mental constructs, collective beliefs, and aggregate perceptions. Several scholars acknowledge the influence of Walter Lippmann (Chen and Meindl 1991; Fombrun and Van Riel 1997; Rindova *et al.* 2006). Lippmann introduced his book *Public Opinion* (1922) by invoking Plato's description of a cave in which prisoners experience reality as a series of shadows cast on the wall. His point was that the real world was out of reach to direct human experience, and that people could have direct experience only of their own "interior representations of the world" (1922: 27). An individual can "see with his mind vast portions of the world that he could never see, touch, smell, hear, or remember," explained Lippmann further. "Gradually he makes for himself a trustworthy picture inside his head of the world beyond his reach" (Lippmann 1922: 29). Lippmann defined public opinions as "the pictures inside the heads of these human beings, the pictures of themselves, of others, of their needs, purposes, and relationship." He reserved the term "Public Opinion with capital letters" for "those pictures which are acted upon by groups of people, or by individuals acting in the name of groups" (1922: 29). Lippmann did not clarify the grounds for the visual metaphors he employed so liberally. But his abstract and aggregate approach to image helped provide the foundation both for public relations as a practice and for the concept of mass society in cultural studies and public opinion research (Ewen 1996; Beniger 1987).

It has become common practice in studies of celebrity to resuscitate Daniel Boorstin's observation that celebrities are people who become famous merely for being famous. In his often-quoted book *The Image: A Guide to Pseudo-Events in America*, Boorstin drew extensively from Lippmann's writings to develop this critique of celebrity culture. But Boorstin maintained that Lippmann's description of "the picture in our heads" no longer captured the complexity of a culture that had been transformed by the very journalistic and public relations practices he had helped to establish. In the new media age, Boorstin argued, images functioned to complexify rather than to simplify reality, if not to supplant it altogether. Media images had become a "thicket of unreality which stands between us and the facts of life," he charged (Boorstin 1961: 3). Boorstin emphasized the centrality of photographs, newsreels, movies, and television to the perpetuation of this "synthetic reality." But he never explored the difference between these visual phenomena and his own more abstract conception of image; nor did he even provide a definition of the term "image" in the book he published by that name.

Organization and leadership scholars often cite both Lippmann and Boorstin as a shorthand way to establish the importance of image in contemporary society while sidestepping visual images altogether (Rindova *et al.* 2005; Gioia *et al.* 2000; Dutton *et al.* 1994; Chen and Meindl 1991). Morgan's (1996) influential work on what he calls "images of organization" reflects this same bias. Morgan defines an image not as an object that we see and interpret, but rather a "way of seeing," an "interpretive construct," or a "metaphor." For Morgan, as for many other authors, the visual image becomes interesting and important only when it becomes a picture in our heads.

The act of seeing functions as an unexamined metaphor for thinking or understanding, and the visual image functions as an unexamined metaphor for metaphor itself.

Only a small minority of scholars in organization and leadership studies have considered image in its concrete and visual sense. A few have explored the significance of photographs in corporate annual reports. Dougherty and Kunda (1990) analyze the annual reports of five major American-based computer firms to highlight the deliberate and self-conscious portrayal of the firms and their relationships with their customers. They argue that the photographs revealed significant differences in the ways that organizational members constructed tacit theories and assumptions about their customers, and conclude that "much can be learned from the contrast of seemingly innocent photographs and the self conscious tales they tell" (1990: 204). In this same vein, Anderson and Imperia (1992) conduct a comparative analysis of photographs of men and women in corporate annual reports. These latter two studies point towards the representational role of photography in the production and consumption of company reports, but do not investigate the deeper ideological and constitutive roles such images can play.

More such research is clearly needed. In order to grapple with the many faces of business celebrity, organization and leadership studies need to develop a refined vocabulary and a theoretical foundation for talking about not just abstract images and the pictures in our heads, but actual visual images and their significance. We have sought to contribute to this effort in a series of published studies on the visual representation of business leadership. We began this research by exploring the relationship between CEO portraits and the notion of authenticity. An understanding of this relationship helps to make clear how business celebrities function more generally as repositories for debates over what it means to be an individual in a corporate society. We therefore summarize this research in the next section.

The corporate quest for authenticity

Our research on the visual representation of business leadership proceeds from the observation that business organizations have a *de facto* image problem. Simply put, they are invisible. No one has ever "seen" an organization or a corporation. You can't take a picture of IBM. This poses a problem, because visible presence has functioned as a traditionally accepted prerequisite for authenticity—a quality widely considered crucial for organizational corporate legitimacy. "The rapid pace of social, political and technological change has clearly increased the consumer's need for *authenticity*," Nestlé CEO Peter Brabeck-Letmathe has declared. "What this means for corporations is quite clear: *presence* and *visibility* are vital in order to build up that capital of trust" (Brabeck-Letmathe 1999, emphasis added). Small wonder, then, that top management figures so often represent their organizations not just in managerial or legal terms, but in visual terms as well. Even as organizations supposedly become more diffuse and less susceptible to visual representation than ever before (Davis and McAdam, 2000), the corporate quest for a human face and the voracious appetite of the business news industries drive the production and circulation of ever more visual images of organizational leadership (Guthey and Jackson 2005).

Our comments in this section are drawn from an article published in 2005 by co-authors Guthey and Jackson entitled "CEO Portraits and the Authenticity Paradox," in which we analyzed the dynamics of this quest through the work of a critically acclaimed Danish photographer of CEOs and other top executives. The photographer we studied, Per Morten Abrahamsen, used a variety of photographic conventions and practices to establish an authentic connection with his subjects. But those very conventions also functioned to highlight the stylized artificiality of both his portraits and the identities they helped to construct. In this same manner, we argued, many CEO portraits appear to project the kind of personal presence that many consider vital for projecting authenticity. But many individual photographs—together with the staggering volume of executive portraiture taken as a whole—focus attention on the constructed nature of photographic representation, corporate self-promotion, and CEO image in ways that render corporate and executive authenticity ever more problematic and elusive.

Neither the quest for corporate authenticity, nor the attempt to use CEO and top executive portraits to create it, are particularly new. Large corporations have always had an image problem, and this problem has always revolved around the issue of authenticity. *Financial Times* columnist Lucy Kellaway (2004) has lampooned the contemporary craze for corporate authenticity as an attempt to control the damage compounded by each new revelation of corporate malfeasance. But the demand for corporate authenticity predates the business scandals of the last several years, even if authenticity has gone by other names in the past. Marchand (1998) points out that one of the first buzzwords associated with the quest for a reassuring human presence and an authentic image was "corporate soul." As corporations began to dominate the American landscape in the early twentieth century, many voiced concern that these strange new institutions had no conscience, no humanizing personality, and no "soul." Large, bureaucratic corporations seemed to threaten the social and economic order not only because of their unprecedented size and power, Marchand explains, but also because they were so abstract, so elusive, and so faceless. "It needs no sleep, it takes no vacations," observed one commentator of the way the corporation appeared to many in the early twentieth century. "If you prick it, it does not bleed. If you tickle it, it does not laugh" (Lustig 1982: 10). Marchand attributes early concerns about the facelessness and soullessness of the corporation to its fragile social and moral legitimacy. He documents how business spokespersons became obsessed with convincing the public that corporations indeed had "souls" in order to shore up that legitimacy, giving birth to corporate image advertising and to the public relations industry in the process.

Goldman and Papson (1996) trace the link between this notion of corporate soul and the contemporary obsession with authenticity. They also stress the centrality of photographs to the project of corporate legitimization. "The power of advertising lies in its ability to photographically frame and redefine our meanings and our experiences and then turn them into meanings that are consonant with corporate interests," they explain. "This power to recontextualize and reframe photographic images has put advertising at the center of contemporary redefinitions of individuality, freedom, and democracy in relation to corporate symbols" (1996: 216). In their analysis of corporate image and identity advertising, Goldman and Papson stress that "the marketing of corporate image usually involves managing visual perceptions of corporate personalities" (1996: 217). Our research has sought to extend this analysis to those personalities at the top of the corporate hierarchy in order to consider how CEO and top executive portraits figure into the visual politics of corporate legitimization.

Goldman and Papson themselves lay important groundwork for this task in their discussion of authenticity and product advertising. They argue that a contradiction at the heart of corporate capitalist culture has transformed authenticity into one of "the most pervasive styles and motifs in our contemporary sign culture" (1996: 140). That contradiction derives from the way consumer culture fragments notions of self, identity, and personhood originally generated from within capitalist culture itself. The rise of market capitalism depended on the construction of a possessive individualism that placed the independent, enterprising, and productive self at the center of the social order (Berman 1970). Fledgling entrepreneurs and industrialists sought to master themselves and their environment, and they measured their success by their ability to leave their mark on the world. "Bourgeois definitions of authenticity stress a self able to project unmediated, spontaneous expressions of personal identity," Goldman and Papson explain (1996: 142). While such ideals may have made sense in a culture predicated on production, they become contradictory in a culture that addresses individuals primarily as consumers. Defined by an endless stream of packaged goods and mediated experiences, consumers find themselves ever more removed from the intensity of direct experience and the ideal of authentic individual identity. "Today authenticity represents the search for individuated space outside the commodity form and outside the spectacle," Goldman and Papson point out (1996: 142). Advertising exacerbates this contradiction by work-ing constantly to co-opt that space, packaging this desire to escape the prison house of consumption in order to promote consumption itself (Frank 1995).

One could argue that a parallel identity crisis among corporations has intensified the quest for corporate authenticity. American legal theory originally defined corporations as "real entities" and bestowed upon them the same rights and (some of) the same duties as "natural persons" (Guthey 2001). But along with other supposedly natural persons, corporations have become more fragmented and diffuse. Downsizing, outsourcing, the stripping away of productive functions, and the governance of corporate activity through increasingly fluid networks, virtual entities, and far-flung financial intermediaries have made corporations extremely difficult to apprehend. "Organization theory traditionally treats corporations as meaningfully bounded, actorly entities analogous to organisms," point out Davis and McAdam. "This was a reasonable imagery for some purposes in analyzing the organization of the post-war American economy, but the metaphors of 'sovereignty' and birth and death no longer make sense of the corporate sector" (2000: 209). They illustrate their point with a description of the tangled web of financial and business arrangements that make up what they call "the entity formerly known as Westinghouse" (2000: 207). Such companies have become more difficult to recognize, let alone visualize. Davis and McAdam caution against exaggerating this break with the past, and Marchand's work makes clear that concerned parties always have had to work hard to make corporations look like anything recognizable at all. Their boundaries, their identity, and their social legitimacy are in constant need of reconstruction and re-authentication.

The authenticity paradox in portrait photography

CEO and top executive photographs play a key role in the processes described above. Recent changes in the organization of corporate activity—however far-reaching—have not diminished the practice of representing that activity via photographs of the meaningfully bounded, actorly entities in charge of it. To the contrary, the number of top executive photographs seems to have multiplied exponentially over the last decade, abetted by the glut of new media outlets and by the amount of corporate communication now conducted via the Internet, the primary communicative language of which is visual (Schroeder 2002). CEO portraits figure so prominently in the visual politics of corporate legitimacy because they appear to reinforce two key qualities commonly associated with authenticity.

The discourse of authenticity often includes the notion that to be authentic means to represent one's self accurately, to be true to one's unique and self-contained identity. It also emphasizes the ability to communicate this individuality and agency through the human capacity for creative self-expression (Goldman and Papson 1996; Frosh 2001). At first glance, portrait photographs deliver both of these key elements of authenticity, since they appear to represent an accurate depiction or visual replica of objective reality, and since they serve up that slice of reality via the creativity of the photographer as an expressive artist. In fact the perceived connection between portraiture, presence, and authenticity predates photography: it was articulated very explicitly by William Hazlitt in the early nineteenth century, and developed by Thomas Carlyle into an argument for the establishment of the National Portrait Gallery in London in 1856 (Barlow 1997).

The authentication of corporate identity by means of CEO portraits parallels the long-standing practice of reinforcing individual identity by means of photographs and portraits. Photographs have been central to the production and reproduction of both individual identities and the modern institution of individual identity writ large. Portraits in particular carve the individual out from the social environment and freeze a fleeting image of identity into a durable icon. For this reason the nascent nineteenth-century bourgeoisie seized upon photographic portraits as a means of establishing the kind of individual identity demanded by a burgeoning market society. "Emerging from traditional society by their own effort, they wanted reinforcement for the point that the unique individual was now important," observes Beloff. "Photography and portrait photographs were ideal means for fulfilling that need" (1985: 22; Tagg 1988). Early portraits and daguerreotypes of busi-

Figure 4.4
Cyrus W. Field, founder
of the Atlantic Telegraph
Company (which became
AT&T). Daguerrotype
from Matthew Brady
Studios, *c.* 1858.

Source: This image is in
the public domain. National
Portrait Gallery,
Smithsonian Institution
(http://www.npg.si.edu/)

ness leaders, like one of AT&T founder Cyrus Field (see Figure 4.4), show
how readily the new technologies of visual representation would lend themselves to the construction of business stature and presence.

The portrait's power to invest individual identity with primacy and
immediacy hinges to a great extent on the perceived connection between
photography and objective reality. Critics from Charles Baudelaire to Lady
Elizabeth Eastlake to Susan Sontag have celebrated photography as the
bearer of "absolute material accuracy," as the "sworn witness to everything
presented to her view," and as "essentially an act of non-intervention" (Wells
1997: 13, 14, 24). Modernist intellectuals in the twentieth century seized
upon these same aspects of photographic technology in their enthusiasm
to leave behind the shackles of traditional values and old world aesthetics.
"Everyone will be compelled to see that which is optically true," declared
Bauhaus artist Moholy-Nagy in the 1920s. "This will abolish that pictorial
and imaginative association pattern which has remained unsuperseded for
centuries and which has been stamped upon our vision by great individual
painters" (Wells 1997: 19). Wells points out that such realist perspectives

celebrate the authenticity of photographs over the artifice of other forms of representation, and that "the authority which emanates from the sense of authenticity or 'truth to actuality' conferred by photography is a fundamental element within photographic language and aesthetics" (Wells 1997: 27).

A countervailing tradition argues that photographs draw their authenticity from their status as expressive art. The introduction of photography in the nineteenth century sparked debates over whether it was a technology or a new art form because "its assumed power of accurate, dispassionate recording appeared to displace the artist's compositional creativity" (Wells 1997: 13; Mirzoeff 1999: 67). Modernists such as Moholy-Nagy transcended this debate by hailing photography as a revolutionary art form precisely *because* of its realist qualities. This perspective survives in the work of critics such as Savedoff, who argues that the photograph's enigmatic power derives from the combination of its perceived realism and its ability to transform its subjects by means of the manipulation of compositional and optical techniques. "Photographs seem to reveal to us things that cannot be seen with our eyes alone," she says. "They have the power to make even the most familiar objects appear strange, the most chaotic events appear structured, or the most mundane items appear burdened with meaning" (Savedoff 2000: 2).

Implicit in this perspective is the image of the artist as a figure who can transform reality, thereby exemplifying the ideals of creativity, autonomy, and achievement that undergird the modern understanding of authenticity. As Goldman and Papson point out, the artist represents the ideal modern self, "able to achieve recognition by projecting himself into the world and transcending the limits of the commodity form" (1996: 151). CEO portraits taken by recognized photographers/artists seek to associate both the executive and the corporation with this ideal artistic self and with his or her own cache of individual personality, authentic human presence, and creative agency. At the same time CEO portraits take advantage of photography's historical association with identity and objective reality to convey the impression that corporations—like CEOs—"*just are*" unique and irreducible entities with all of the expressive characteristics conventionally ascribed to authentic individuals.

Upon closer inspection, neither CEOs nor portrait photographs just are—they turn out to be just as "authenticity-challenged" as corporations. CEOs may appear as exemplary and enterprising individuals who present themselves directly and personally on magazine and book covers, websites, and the pages of annual reports. But it takes a massive rhetorical and representational effort, as well as a collective leap of faith, for these individuals plausibly to stand in for the ever-shifting web of commercial activities, financial arrangements, and mediated ownership structures we call corporations (Guthey 1997, 2001, 2004; Czarniawska 1997; Khurana 2002a and 2002b). This is so both because no individual can bear the representational burden of personifying the complexity of corporate activity, and, more fundamentally, because individual identity itself, like corporate identity, is a socially constructed institution that requires constant care and maintenance. As we will discuss in the next chapter, the current climate of recrimination and backlash against formerly deified CEOs such as Jack Welch and Dennis Kozlowski foregrounds the fragile and contingent nature of CEO identity, since conflicting images and/or photographs of the same celebrity CEO—as a victorious business titan *and* as a shameless or even criminal profiteer—suggest that both images are socially determined constructions (Chen and Meindl 1991; Guthey and Jackson 2003).

The stylistic evolution of portrait photographs reflects a growing emphasis on the constructed nature of human identity and on photography's complicity in constructing it. Although the renowned Canadian photographer Yousuf Karsh carefully composed his mid-twentieth-century portraits of famous persons, including business titans, he insisted that the camera had the power "to stir the emotions of the viewer" and to "lay bare the soul" of the subject, thus revealing his or her true inner self. But as the twentieth century wore on, portrait photographers began to deconstruct this imperative to "unmask" or capture a definitive image of the self. Many post-war portrait photographers, most notably Richard Avedon, Diane Arbus, Robert Mapplethorpe, and Cindy Sherman, have made the problem of identity basic to their work, turning away from the "inner self" and focusing instead on the mask and on the glittering surfaces of photographic staging and composition. Annie Liebovitz exemplifies the communicative power of such highly self-conscious staging in the portraits of famous celebrities she produced for the covers of *Rolling Stone* and *Vanity Fair* in the 1970s and 1980s (Liebovitz 1983).

Ironically, many such photographers contribute to the perception of their own authentic artistic identity by foregrounding the staged and therefore problematic nature of authentic identity in their photographs. While many do so in a playful manner or for popular commercial effect, the practice points to a more serious challenge to the assumed connection between photographic representation and authenticity. To be contrived and staged stands for the opposite of what it means to be authentic. On a more fundamental level, such self-conscious attention to stylistic and compositional elements brings to the fore what is fundamentally photographic and even mechanical about portrait photography. According to Benjamin, the mechanical ability to reproduce endless copies of any photographic negative (or digital image file) eradicates the very possibility of authenticity. "The presence of the original is the prerequisite to the concept of authenticity," said Benjamin. "Even the most perfect reproduction of a work of art is lacking in one element: its presence in time and space, its unique existence at the place where it happens to be" (Benjamin 2003: 43). Far from establishing an authentic presence, then, from this perspective the portrait photograph by its very nature diminishes the presence and the authority of both the photographer and the subject.

The authenticity paradox and the celebrity industries

The celebrity industries have heightened the authenticity paradox inherent in portrait photography by cultivating the practice of digitally retouching media images of celebrities to the point where it is no longer possible to trust that any photograph of a well known figure has not been tampered with. Pascal Dangin is the most prominent of the "digital intermediaries" who perform this now nearly obligatory service. "Around thirty celebrities keep him on retainer, in order to insure that any portrait of them that appears in any outlet passes through his shop, to be scrubbed of crow's-feet and stray hairs," reports the *New Yorker* magazine in the spring of 2008. "Dangin's company, Box Studios, has eighty employees and occupies a four-story warehouse in the meatpacking district (in New York City)." Dangin also works closely and regularly with renowned photographers like Annie Leibovitz, Steven Meisel, and Mario Sorrenti, as well as with magazines such as *Vanity Fair*, *Harper's Bazaar*, and *Allure*. In one issue of *Vogue* alone Dangin manipulated 144 images, including the cover photo of Drew Barrymore. This factory mode of production lends credence to Dangin's own claim that "the only public figure whose image tends not to be manipulated is the Queen" (Collins 2008).

One might argue that candid photographs, including the kind of paparazzi images intended to make celebrities look bad, instead of good, are not constructed, staged, and manipulated in this manner, so that they do therefore offer a direct link to what celebrity figures are really like. But actually, this possibility has been eliminated by the manner in which the celebrity system has swallowed up the very notion of "candid reality" and transformed it into an industrial product. An article in *The Atlantic* magazine in April, 2008 called the Hollywood paparazzi "one of the most powerful and lucrative forces driving the American news-gathering industry," and detailed how a business model developed over the last eight years or so has transformed the hunt for candid photos of celebrities from a highly individualistic business into a cross between a professional team contact sport and a sausage factory (Samuels 2008). According to the author, the industrial phase of paparazzi photo production began when agencies such as X17 and Bauer-Griffin figured out that the ever-proliferating number of new media outlets, magazines, and Internet blogs meant that they could make more money from selling batches of celebrity pictures many times over to all interested parties than they could from cutting exclusive deals with high-profile publications such as *People* or *Us*. With this in mind, X17's owner François Navarre equipped whole gangs of young, fearless would-be photographers with digital cameras and sent them out to hunt down the likes of Britney Spears and Brad Pitt. Many of Navarre's "shooters" were recent immigrants who had never taken a picture in their life, but they provided a cheap labor force that could swarm around celebrities anywhere, anytime, often disregarding the law as well as their own and others' personal safety.

Standard practice in this industry is to bear down on celebrity "targets" from several sides at once, so that when they look away from one shooter, they automatically face another one. As *The Atlantic* reports, it is not uncommon for thirty or forty paparazzi to "work" a celebrity like Britney Spears at one time. Agencies carefully scrutinize the many thousands of photos produced in this manner to select the best ones to circulate. Caught in the crosshairs of such an aggressively industrialized form of celebrity big game hunting, some celebrities choose to "give it up" and cooperate with the shooters to stage the best photograph possible for their own purposes. But even those that choose to fight back or run are not being photographed in their "natural habitat." Instead they are participating in an elaborately staged media ritual intended, paradoxically, to mass produce images of celebrities when they are not on stage. In this manner the industrialized nature of paparazzi photo production highlights the fact that there is literally nothing about the celebrity system that is not the result of a heavily populated process of social construction.

The constructed nature of portrait photographs and the industrialized production of paparazzi snapshots together help to exemplify both the direct and the metaphorical links between visual images of business celebrity and the phenomenon of business celebrity writ large. In a direct sense, visual images are crucial to the construction of business celebrity, because they provide the means for holding out the promise of direct, unmediated relationships with important business figures and the organizations or business dynamics they represent. But like the phenomenon of celebrity itself, photographs of important business celebrities cannot deliver on this promise. To paraphrase again Rojek's argument from the last chapter, both celebrities and photographs of celebrities promote a form of abstract desire that can never be fulfilled. This is so because business celebrities are not simply exemplary individuals with whom one can have a relationship, and because photographs of business celebrities are not just direct, visual representations of such individuals. Both are the end product of an elaborate and overcrowded industrial process, and the relational dynamics of that process exert considerable influence over the celebrities and the celebrity images that it produces.

In the previous chapter we built upon this same insight to develop a new approach to business celebrities. In the concluding section of this chapter we will describe also how we have developed an aesthetic and interpretive approach to visual images of business leaders and celebrities as sites of dialogue, debate, and open conflict over the nature of business leadership and the notion of what it means to be a person in a corporate society.

A relational aesthetics of business celebrity

In order for the photographic representation of CEOs and other business celebrities to figure into the ever-expanding research literature on organizational and leadership image, we have argued, scholars in these fields will have to loosen their dependence on the certainty of social scientific methods, and open up to aesthetic insights and interpretive methodologies from the humanities, from art history, and from photography theory and criticism (Strati 1992; Strati and Guillet de Montoux 2002). But leadership and organization studies do not come to this table empty handed, because images of business celebrities are not merely aesthetic phenomena. Like business celebrities themselves, they are also products of intersecting processes of social and industrial interaction, involving a variety of corporate actors and cultural intermediaries—photographers, communications and public relations staff, photo editors, graphic designers, digital artists, journalists, and other concerned parties—all of whom pursue overlapping and sometimes conflicting agendas and interests. Social interaction also characterizes the exhibition, consumption, and interpretation of images of business celebrity. Rosenblum (1978) has argued that even the aesthetic aspects of photographic style represent forms of social process and interaction. Organization and leadership studies can build on their existing strengths to explore further the social and organizational dynamics that lead to the production and distribution of so many images of business celebrities and top executives.

Co-authors Guthey and Jackson have contributed to this effort by developing an aesthetic and interpretive approach to images of business celebrity and leadership that foregrounds the interaction of multiple meanings (Guthey and Jackson 2008). We developed our approach by means of an analysis of two photo illustrations of Carly Fiorina that appeared in the *New York Times* after her ouster as CEO of Hewlett Packard in February, 2005. We do not reproduce these images here for copyright reasons. In fact, the minefield of copyright restrictions, especially when it comes to the ever more lucrative market for images of celebrities, turns the publication of research into this topic into a considerable challenge. The two illustrations of Fiorina can be viewed on the *New York Times* website (see Bilton 2005; Cenicola and Best 2005). In our analysis we described these two images as *metapictures*, borrowing theorist W.J.T. Mitchell's term for a special class of images best understood as pictures of pictures (Mitchell 1995). Metapictures are instructive because they provide a visual depiction of the very representational conventions according to which images produce meaning. With this in mind we used the Fiorina illustrations to isolate three analytic categories that can help to highlight the relational and multivalent characteristics of media images of business celebrities such as Fiorina—*frame*, *gaze*, and *period eye*.

Attention to the presence of frames in and around a photograph or image can help foreground the multiple ways in which images can be viewed and interpreted. In this regard it is important to think of frames not simply as the natural edges or borders of an image, even though frames conventionally point away from themselves and towards the visual content they contain. On second glance, the existence of a frame points towards choices made about what to include in an image, and what to exclude from it. These choices often have ideological consequences, because they sublimate conflicts over what might have otherwise been included. The images that the *New York Times* used to accompany the coverage of Carly Fiorina's ouster were particularly interesting in this regard, because they contained multiple frames within frames, thereby foregrounding the conflict between different interpretations of Fiorina's image. We also argued that these frames within frames pointed very self-consciously towards the media representation of exemplary business figures such as Fiorina, thereby both participating in and calling into question the process of business celebrification at the same time. As we concluded, attention to frames helps make clear the social and interactive nature of visual images of business celebrity—"because the framing of any image is not a natural occurrence but a conscious choice; because there are multiple visible or implicit instances of such choices in any image; and because these various choices can interact and conflict with each other" (Guthey and Jackson 2008: 87).

While frames objectify, we have argued, gazes subjectify. That is, the notion of the gaze emphasizes the act of looking instead of the state of framed "to-be-looked-at-ness." Visual and media theorists have used the word "gaze" as a technical term that effectively conveys John Berger's notion that "every image embodies a way of seeing" (1972: 10). A way of seeing or gaze embodied in a photograph points towards the subject position and agency of the person doing the seeing. In their study of *National Geographic Magazine*, Lutz and Collins added to this argument the important qualification that even individual photographs function as sites where many ways of seeing intersect. The intersecting gazes they found in *National Geographic* photographs included the photographer's; the magazine editors'; the readers'; the non-western subjects'; the gaze of westerners portrayed within the frame looking at non-westerners; and even the academic gaze (Lutz and Collins 1993). Their main point was that the intersection of these many gazes turns photographs into sites where meaning and power relations are constantly renegotiated. We have found this latter insight useful because images of business celebrity also function as sites where gazes intersect, including those of media consumers, board members, employees, investors, competitors, regulators, and other media outlets. These viewing agents all have different interests and preconceptions. For this reason they can frame the celebrity in overlapping, divergent, or even conflicting ways, thus making it impossible to interpret any given celebrity in only one way. From this we conclude that any given image does not merely embody a certain way of seeing. Even an individual image embodies *multiple ways of seeing*, and constant interaction between them.

But the ways of seeing embodied in a photograph are not unlimited. The social and multivalent dynamics of visual representation do not imply that images of business celebrities can mean anything at all. To emphasize the limits and pressures placed on the interpretation of any image, we have invoked art historian Michael Baxandall's concept of the "period eye." According to Baxandall, contextual and historical information is crucial to understanding the pictorial style of visual images. Conversely, visual images provide important clues for reconstructing the "distinctive social experiences" out of which pictorial styles and visual habits evolve. The period eye is therefore a set of socially embedded visual habits and learned predispositions towards interpreting visual cues in certain ways. When looking at images through the period eye, Baxandall says, the mind brings three kinds of culturally relative resources to bear on the interpretation of an image—"a stock of patterns, categories and methods of inference; training in a range of representational conventions; and experience, drawn from the environment, in what are plausible ways of visualizing what we have incomplete information about" (Baxandall 1988: 32). Baxandall goes out of his way to make clear that these habits and predispositions do not simply determine that any given image can only be interpreted in one way during a particular historical moment, because "each of us has had different experiences, and so each of us has slightly different knowledge and skills of interpretation" (1988: 29).

We can demonstrate how these interpretive lenses help us appreciate the complexity of the visual representation of business celebrity by directing them towards an intriguing photograph that was taken during Bill Gates' trip to Hanoi, Vietnam, in April, 2006. The *New York Times* published the photo alongside an article entitled "Communist Vietnam Lunges for the Capitalist Brass Ring" (Mydans 2006). Although it was Lenin's birthday, and the Communist Party was holding its most important meeting in five years, the article pointed out, "the star of the show was the world's most famous capitalist, Bill Gates." The newspaper described the scene further:

> The president, the prime minister and the deputy prime minister all excused themselves from the party meeting on Saturday to have their pictures taken with Mr. Gates, who has more star power in Vietnam than any of them.
>
> When people heard he was in town, hundreds climbed trees and pushed through police lines to get a glimpse of him. He was the subject of the lead article in the next day's newspapers.
>
> "That was very symbolic," said Le Dang Doanh, an official in the Ministry of Planning, speaking of the reception for Mr. Gates. "It is a very clear sign of the new mood of society and the people. Everybody wants to be like Bill Gates."
>
> (Mydans 2006)

The photograph that ran with this article was taken by Associated Press photographer Richard Vogel. In the center of the photograph was 21-year-old computer engineering student Le Tuan Anh, standing in the middle of a crowd of his fellow students. He holds over his head a copy of *Saigon Entrepreneur*, which sports a large photo of a smiling Bill Gates on its cover. "I've been waiting for Bill Gates to come to Vietnam for a long time," commented Le Tuan Anh in a separate press release from the Associated Press. "Hopefully this will boost IT development in Vietnam" (Tran 2006).

The image fascinates on a number of levels, and exemplifies the intersecting dynamics of attribution, traction, mediation, and access we have located at the heart of the celebrity phenomenon (see Figure 4.5). Like the images of Carly Fiorina described above, this photograph contains several frames within frames. Counting them from the inside out, Bill Gates himself is framed by the cover photograph, which is in turn framed by the masthead and confines of the *Saigon Entrepreneur*. The student holds his arms up straight, forming what ends up looking like a very square frame around the newspaper. His expression is somber or contemplative, but he is framed by the many other students smiling and laughing around him. Of course, this whole scene is framed by the photographer's decisions on how to compose and crop the photo, which is again framed by the *New York Times* article, as well as the rest of the editorial decisions made by the staff of the newspaper that day, not to mention the visual confines of the *Times* archive web page where the article and photograph still remain available (Mydans 2006).

Figure 4.5 Vietnamese students thronging to see Bill Gates (Vogel 2006).

Source: Reproduced with the permission of AP/Polfoto, and with thanks to photographer Richard Vogel

These many frames help to accentuate precisely what is at first most eye-catching about this photograph—the interplay of overlapping contexts in which Bill Gates' image comes into play. It is the fact that *communist Vietnam* celebrates the arrival of the world's premier *American capitalist* that initially causes one's head to turn. But the earnest fervor with which the student at the center of the photo holds up his image of Bill Gates also commands attention. He clearly frames Bill Gates as an important figure *for him*, and attributes to Gates the qualities that he admires. One does not have to read too much into this photograph to interpret it as an image of hope and aspiration. In this manner this photograph accentuates our point that the activities of consumers and fans are crucial for the construction and maintenance of business celebrity, because it is only when a business figure gains such traction that we can actually call him or her a celebrity. The fact that Gates has such traction even on the streets of Hanoi attests to the global reach of his celebrity veneer.

While the grass-roots enthusiasm that Bill Gates can generate in far-flung locations around the world is clearly very palpable in this photograph, it is also important to remember that both the photograph itself *and* the photograph Le Tuan Anh holds above his head are produced and framed by the commercial media—by the AP photographer, by the photographer of the image on the cover of *Saigon Entrepreneur*, and by the editors of every subsequent publication and web page on which this image appears. This reinforces our point about the central role of business culture intermediaries in the celebrity phenomenon. The media stand between Le Tuan Anh and Bill Gates. They function as gatekeepers and they frame the relationship between the student and the computer mogul. For this reason it is also important to note that the multiple frames in this image keep Bill Gates far out of reach. The students are on hand to get close to the "real" Bill Gates "in person." But the photograph depicts only the students getting close to yet another media representation of Bill Gates. In a certain sense, therefore, this photograph drives home the point that these students will never have direct or intimate access to Bill Gates, in spite of the fact that the promise of such access was what clearly motivated many thousands of Vietnamese people to greet him upon his arrival in the first place.

It's not clear that the students in this photograph would be all that crestfallen if confronted with this last comment. Most of them appear to be enjoying themselves regardless, gazing off in many different directions as if to accentuate the point that there are many pleasures to be derived from celebrity events, and that several of these pleasures don't hinge upon a private word or a handshake with the guest of honor himself or herself. A variety of different gazes criss-cross and intersect in this photograph, because there are many different ways to view such an event, and many different ways to view celebrity figures like Bill Gates. From this perspective the photograph itself is about the appropriation and use of Bill Gates' image by a variety of different people for a variety of different purposes. By holding up a media image of Bill Gates, Le Tuan Anh makes a statement about his aspirations, about his place in the social order, and about his relationship to Bill Gates, to his fellow students, to his country, and to his own future. Using the image of a very prominent business celebrity, he enters into a dialogue about what it means to be Bill Gates, what it means to be Le Tuan Anh, and what it means to be a person in a modern society dominated by powerful business institutions.

The business celebrity eye

We have suggested that the analysis of CEO portraits and other images of business celebrities call for the development of what we might term the "corporate capitalist eye" or the "business media eye." For the purposes of this book we might coin yet another, related term, the "business celebrity eye." By means of this concept we mean to emphasize that in order to understand why there are so many pictures of a figure like Bill Gates in circulation, and in order to understand the meaning of individual images like the one discussed above, we need to cultivate a certain sensitivity for approaching such images. This requires the ability to recognize the poses, props, and visual cues that have become commonplace in the representation of business leaders. It also requires an appreciation of the stylistic conventions that govern the portrayal not only of business figures, but also of celebrities more generally, and an understanding of what is going on when these conventions get mixed together. Finally, an eye for the visual representation of business celebrities requires a grasp of some of the issues we have sought to introduce in this chapter. It requires insight into the complex dynamics at play when photographs of individual persons are used to represent complex organizations and business dynamics.

In a certain sense, of course, anyone living in our media- and corporation-saturated society has grown up with just such a sensitivity, to the point where images of business leaders and celebrities do not even raise an eyebrow. We see such images all the time, and they don't seem strange or complex at all. This is what John Tagg means when he states that "the transparency of the photograph is its most powerful rhetorical device" (Tagg 1988: 35). We all think we know what photographs represent, and what they mean. Through repeated exposure, portrait photographs and celebrity snapshots of business leaders have gained acceptance as natural and accurate means of representing what we think of as straightforward individual and organizational identities. For this very reason, however, Tagg insists that photographs deserve more critical scrutiny, so that we can understand *how* they represent and signify what they do. As he puts it, "this rhetoric has a history, and we must distance ourselves from it, question the naturalness of portraiture and probe the obviousness of each image" (Ibid.). Attention to the conventions that govern the business celebrity eye can help make them strange again, and bring to the surface taken-for-granted assumptions about their significance.

This is where our exercise in cataloging some of the nearly one-and-a-half million images of Bill Gates can come in handy. The first point one notices when dipping into the vast ocean of Bill Gates imagery is of course the sheer number of images available out there. A Google image search for "Bill Gates" produces a seemingly endless series of results pages that can be characterized visually as multiple frames within frames. Like the images of Carly Fiorina that we discussed earlier, these provide a graphic illustration of the fact that a figure like Gates is constantly framed, looked at, and understood from a variety of different and often irreconcilable interpretive and ideological points of view. The images range from the fairly sophisticated to the extremely childish, from the obsequiously fawning to the downright insulting. It is simply not possible to reconcile images of Gates as a brown-shirted Nazi with images of Bill Gates as a caring philanthropist holding a young African child, nor is it possible to boil down these many visual representations into something we could refer to collectively as "Bill Gates' media image."

Gates is somewhat of a special case in this regard, because his likeness has become so ubiquitous that it functions as a sort of a free-floating signifier, instantly recognizable and available for appropriation in a seemingly infinite number of ways. The image of Gates crossing the Delaware with which we opened this chapter is a fine case in point. It was produced by artist and graphic designer Daniel Sroka as an entry to an informal contest sponsored by the technology blog Gizmodo.com in 2007. The feature was titled "Bill Gates (Degraded) Throughout History: Photoshop Gallery of Glory." Entries included digitally altered images of Gates as Jesus Christ, Lee Harvey Oswald, John Lennon, and Genghis Khan, among others, and transported him into such famous events as the signing of the Treaty of Yalta, the fall of the Berlin Wall, the battle of Iwo Jima, the War of 1812, and the Last Supper. Some of the images can be interpreted as witty satire on Gates' celebrity status. Others are just silly ideas or jokes made possible by the wonders of Photoshop. The overall effect of the sixty-six images in the feature is to reinforce the sassy and irreverent tone of the website, which like many technology blogs seems to mix a certain amount of resentment of Bill Gates' power and wealth with a grudging resentment of his contributions to the world of computers.

These and many other digitally altered images of Bill Gates also reinforce our point that individual business celebrities don't have "an image." They have multiple, often conflicting images. Taken as a whole, the iconographic representation of Bill Gates as either a force for good or a force for evil, as a menacing monopolist or a friendly philanthropist, as a dangerous capitalist or a harmless computer geek, tells us very little about what Gates the person "is really like." Instead these many images of Gates provide a map of the contours of a series of debates about Gates, about Microsoft, about the concentration of power in the computer industry, and about the proper nature and function of the corporation in a democratic society and a globalized world. In this sense the elaborately staged representational struggle over Gates' image has little to do with the "real Bill Gates" and everything to do with cultural tensions and debates over corporate authority, individual agency, technological innovation, and antitrust. As we mentioned in the first chapter, the Robber Barons of the late nineteenth century prefigured Gates by embodying many of these same tensions and debates themselves. But the "business celebrity eye" necessary to understand visual images of a Rockefeller or a Carnegie is different from the one needed to understand the many faces of Bill Gates. Technologies have evolved, regulatory and cultural landscapes have shifted, and the media industries have revolutionized themselves several times over. As a result, the representational practices associated with both business leaders and celebrities have changed.

The shifting ways in which business celebrities are represented in the media point to the shifting nature of debates about the proper place and function of business institutions in contemporary society. Struggles over how important business figures are represented constitute struggles over exactly who should run those institutions, how those institutions should be run, and how much power they should have. These struggles become most noticeable when celebrities rise and fall, as they inevitably do. In the next chapter, we explore how the multivalent and dialogic nature of business celebrity constructions— in both visual forms and otherwise—helps to account for the cyclical nature of CEO popularity and the recurrent media phenomenon we have called the CEO celebrity backlash.

5 Open season

The perennial backlash against business celebrities

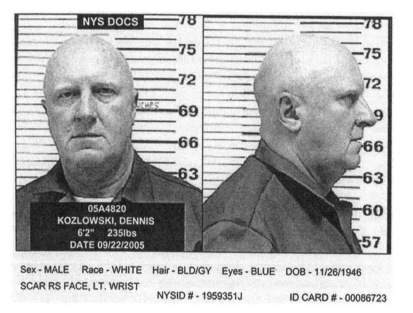

Figure 5.1 Former Tyco CEO Dennis Kozlowski upon admission to the maximum security Downstate Correctional Facility in Fishkill, New York, in September, 2005.

Source: This image is in the public domain. *The Smoking Gun* (http://thesmokinggun.com)

In the previous chapter we made the point that the production and circulation of photographs and other visual images contribute substantially to the aura surrounding business celebrities, and to the kind of rapt fascination that, for example, would lead cheering crowds of thousands to turn out to catch a glimpse of Bill Gates even in a far corner of the world like Hanoi. But we certainly do not want to imply that visual images of business celebrities always elevate them to the status of heroes to be emulated, that the media invariably treat business celebrities in a positive manner, or that widespread attention paid to business celebrities stems exclusively from the general public's unflagging admiration for their achievements and acumen. In fact, our emphasis on the multiplicity of celebrity images in circulation, and on the multiple meanings that get attached to those images, implies just the opposite. For every person that reveres Bill Gates as a great business leader, there seems to be another who despises him as a power-hungry monopolist. He is not the most visible business figure in the world merely because computer engineering students from Houston to Hanoi all love him, or love the idea of him. The media frenzy for all things Bill Gates is also driven by the fact that so many people love to hate him, or simply hate the very idea of him.

This kind of antipathy toward Bill Gates, toward other business celebrities, and toward the idea of business celebrities in general is not restricted to obscure websites with names like "Microsucks." (We are not making this up. There are actually more than one of these. One sports the subheading, "What do you want to monopolize today?" and features prominently in its masthead a picture of Bill Gates taken just after someone threw a pie in his face. Another targets a more highbrow audience with articles like "Fuck You Microsoft." See Microsucks, 2008a and 2008b.) The mainstream media also participate in this kind of business celebrity bashing on a regular, one might even say continuous basis, albeit in a slightly less juvenile manner. In fact these latter sources often take the argument a step further, concluding from the misfortunes of this or that business celebrity that the whole idea of business celebrity itself has overstayed its welcome.

Elsewhere we have written about what we have termed the CEO celebrity backlash, a phenomenon whereby the business news media declare that the heyday of the business celebrity is finished, that everyone is tired of such self-aggrandizing figures, and that it is time for top executives to stop playing rock star and get back to business basics (Jackson and Guthey 2006). In this chapter we will expand upon that idea to discuss the dark underside of the celebrification process. Our point is that attacks on individual business celebrities and media pronouncements about the end of the business celebrity era writ large can have the opposite of their ostensibly intended effect, instead contributing directly to the phenomenon of business celebrity. Celebrity bashing is an integral and necessary part of the construction of celebrity. The urge to knock the powerful off their pedestals stokes the flames of an obsessive fascination with celebrity figures just as much as, if not more than, adoration of them does. Celebrification depends crucially on de-celebrification.

There are several reasons why this is the case. From the kind of industrial perspective we developed in Chapter 2, the rise and fall of specific business celebrities can be understood as a mechanism for product differentiation, or as a form of planned obsolescence. Given the importance of intermediaries and gatekeepers to the functioning of the celebrity industries, an industrial perspective also can choose to interpret the ever changing fortunes of business celebrities as the result of intense competition and jostling for position among celebrity industry players over which figures will remain on top, or over whose product will receive the most positive spin. In both instances an industrial perspective emphasizes that the media exercise considerable power over the fate of business celebrities. But as the proliferation of "Microsucks," "Punch Bill Gates," and other such websites helps makes clear, it is important to remember that audiences also contribute enthusiastically to the savaging and denigration of business celebrities.

Speaking from a broader, cultural studies perspective, several theorists argue that the very media power that generates fascination with celebrities also can foster considerable resentment, leading audiences to exert their own power by lashing back at them as well. This kind of reaction to media power reflects a more general cultural ambivalence over the power that certain individuals can gain by rising to the top of business institutions, and over the influence that large corporations exert over modern society. The backlash reaction against business celebrities exemplifies the manner in which such figures can function as flashpoints for debates and conflicts over what business leadership should be like, and over what it means to be a person in a society dominated by business institutions.

In order to pursue these issues further we begin this chapter with a more extensive description of the phenomenon we have called the CEO celebrity backlash. As we make clear, it is a widespread phenomenon that involves not only news outlets but also mass-market books, academic research, law enforcement efforts, grass-roots websites and blogs, and even film and television productions. The backlash often manifests itself as a distinctively visual phenomenon, mobilizing a variety of images, mug shots, and especially digitally altered photographs to put business celebrities back in their place. A staple ingredient of the backlash is the characterization of the downfall of business celebrities as an unprecedented and radical departure from the normal state of celebration and adulation which such figures have grown to expect. But we want to make clear that the backlash is a recurrent phenomenon, and that in this sense it echoes some of the central features of the management fashion phenomenon as discussed in Chapter 3. In the second section of this chapter we therefore draw out the connections between the business celebrity backlash and the dynamics of management fashions. We argue that the backlash is both a rhetorical device or cliché that gets mobilized by various management fashions, as well as a minor management fashion in its own right.

In the third section of this chapter we turn to the work of theorists in cultural studies in order to discuss the centrality of the backlash to the phenomenon of celebrity itself. These sources emphasize that the kind of profound ambivalence towards celebrity figures exemplified by the backlash stems from the structural dynamics of how celebrity actually works its magic and maintains its hold on the public imagination, both as an industry and as a cultural phenomenon. We conclude this chapter with a discussion of the connections between this kind of ambivalence and what Guthey elsewhere has called "anti-managerialism," an ideological strain in American business culture that both criticizes and legitimizes top managerial power at the same time (Guthey 2004). As we discuss in Chapter 6, the complex cultural and ideological dynamics of business celebrity bashing exert considerable influence over discussions about the proper nature and function of leadership. In the context of such discussions, the celebrity perspective we have developed in this book can provide a deeper understanding of both heroic approaches to leadership and more recent attempts on the part of a number of leadership scholars to explore a variety of alternative, post-heroic approaches.

The CEO celebrity backlash

> Kozlowski vows Tyco's earnings will once again grow by more than 20% a year. That would bring him closer to his ultimate goal: inheriting the mantle once worn by Jack Welch.
>
> *(BusinessWeek 2002)*

> Tyco's former CEO will be remembered as one of the great corporate hoodwinkers.
>
> (Symonds 2002)

> Rogues at companies like WorldCom and Enron were bad enough, but even superstar executives like Jack Welch contributed to the staining of corporate America.
>
> (O'Neal 2002)

In 2002 the business media declared "open season" on high-profile CEOs. The shift from the celebratory, party atmosphere of the dot.com era towards the widespread recrimination against CEO celebrities and hero business leaders was plain to see across a range of media and publications, primarily in the popular business press, but also in statements made by corporate officials themselves, by government officials, and, significantly, by business academics. We have chosen to describe this phenomenon as a "backlash." The *New World Dictionary of the American Language* defines a backlash as "a quick, sharp recoil" as well as "any sudden or violent reaction [such as a] strong political or social reaction resulting from fear or resentment of a movement, candidate, etc." The CEO backlash represented just such a strong negative reaction against the period of exuberant CEO hero worship and celebration that coincided with the New Economy era and the stock market bubble of the 1990s. The very pundits and media outlets that had fueled the engines of CEO hype throughout that period suddenly seemed to delight in ridiculing many of the same CEOs as mendacious and self-serving, if not outright criminal.

The transformation from the New Economy heyday of CEO celebrity to the post-Enron era of disillusionment and finger-pointing seemed to have occurred almost overnight—precipitated by the bursting of the dot.com bubble and the continuing cascade of revelations about corporate scandal, insider trading, and executive wrongdoing, and exacerbated by the tensions and uncertainties brought on by the terrorist attacks of September 11, 2001. The contrast between these before-and-after moments is particularly jarring when one considers how much the conventional wisdom about individual CEO hero figures changed—they could do no wrong one day, and they became symbols of all that is corrupt about corporate activity the next. Even the seemingly untouchable Jack Welch, former chair and chief executive of General Electric, suffered this fate. In the divorce battle precipitated by his extramarital affair with *Harvard Business Review* editor Suzy Wetlaufer, his then-wife Jane Beasley Welch filed papers revealing the full extent of the compensation and retirement package he had received from GE. The scandal eventually led to an SEC investigation, and led Welch to return significant portions of his perks to the company as well (Murray *et al.* 2002). The whole episode tarnished the image of the man once touted by *Fortune* magazine as "The Manager of the Century" (Colvin 1999).

The Economist commented on Welch's media come-uppance in visual form with a cover illustration depicting a toppled statue of the former GE leader. "The world is falling out of love with celebrity chief executives," the story inside declared. "Business leaders are being knocked off their pedestals faster than Communist heroes after the fall of the Berlin Wall" (2002: 11). *The Economist* explained the vehemence of the reaction against the former idols of the boom years as a function of three primary factors: the dramatic plunge in stock prices over which contemporary CEOs had presided; the widespread perception of their unbounded personal greed during this same period of decline; and the excess with which they had been celebrated over the previous decade or so. "Revolutions devour their children, and the impact of new technology and the bull market on business was little short of a revolution," observed the magazine. "Now for the devouring" (*The Economist* 2002: 11).

Virtually all of the popular business media joined in the feast, perhaps none with more relish than *Fortune Magazine*. In November 2002, *Fortune* published a special issue on "CEOs under Fire: Inside the World of Today's Embattled Chief Executives." The lead story was titled "From Heroes to Goats . . . and Back Again? How Corporate Leaders Lost Our Trust" (Useem 2002). The authors felt compelled to remind readers that "there was a time, believe it or not, when CEOs weren't regarded as a threat to children. Bookstores brimmed with titles like How to Become CEO, How to Act Like a CEO, The Mind of the CEO, and, oh, yes, CEO Logic: How to Think and Act Like a Chief Executive. We got ourselves a whole White House full of CEOs." The root cause of the current CEO crisis, *Fortune* charged, was that CEOs had "co-opted the rhetoric of shareholder value and perverted it to their own ends." *Fortune* articles and cover stories from earlier in the year make clear that the special issue on the embattled CEO was not a one-time concession. Alongside the requisite "Managers of the Year" and "Most Admired Companies" issues (Diba and Munoz, 2001), *Fortune* ran stories with decidedly less celebratory and more alarming titles: "The Insiders: You Bought, They Sold" (Gimein *et al.* 2002); "System Failure: Corporate America, We Have a Crisis" (Nocera 2002); and "Send Them to Jail," the sub-heading of which declared "They lie they cheat they steal and they've been getting away with it for too long") (Leaf 2002). Newspapers around the world chimed in with headlines like "Reining in the Imperial CEO" (Leonhardt and Sorkin 2002), "How Celebrity CEOs Failed to Deliver" (*Toronto Star* 2002), "Time We Got Uber the Mensch Thing" (Shand 2002), and "CEO: (*n*) Greedy Liar with Personality Disorder" (Skapinker 2003). Always willing to lend its particular brand of hyperbole to any trend, *Fast Company* magazine contributed to the backlash frenzy with a story entitled "The Secret Life of the CEO: Do They Even Know Right from Wrong?" (Hammonds 2002).

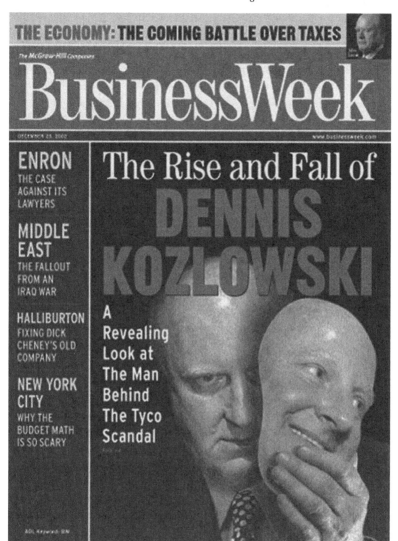

Figure 5.2 The rise and fall of Dennis Kozlowski. *BusinessWeek* cover from December 23, 2002.

Source: http://www.businessweek.com

As these many sources illustrate, from within the perspective of the backlash it appeared puzzling that so many individuals, institutions, and media outlets could have been fooled by all of the ne'er-do-well CEOs and their schemes for so long. A case in point is *BusinessWeek*'s treatment of the erstwhile chief executive of Tyco Corporation, Dennis Kozlowski, who was indicted on charges of fraud in 2002, and eventually sentenced to between eight and twenty-five years in prison. "How DidThey Miss a Scam So Big?" *BusinessWeek* demanded of theTyco Corporation's board of directors soon after the scandal broke, conveniently failing to mention that just eight months earlier the magazine itself had celebrated the now-dishonored ex-Tyco chief Dennis Kozlowski as one of its twenty-five "Managers of the Year." The cover of the December 23, 2002 issue of the magazine exemplifies this blaring contradiction (Figure 5.2). A photo illustration displays an ominous Dennis Kozlowski, lurking behind a smiling mask, while the accompanying text promises "A Revealing Look at the Man Behind theTyco Scandal" (Bianco *et al.* 2002).

The Kozlowski cover image provides perhaps the ultimate visual representation of the profound ambivalence inherent in the CEO celebrity backlash, and highlights some of the important features of backlash images more generally. By portraying in visual form the stripping away of the mask of celebrity artifice, the image emphasizes the centrality of *access* to the construction of the celebrity aura. As we discussed in Chapter 2, the process of celebrification depends in large part on the notion that the media offer audiences a sort of backstage pass, a glimpse at the truth about what celebrities are really like behind the scenes of fabrication and artifice. A prime example of this is the media circulation of actual mug shots like the one of Kozlowski himself at the beginning of this chapter (see Figure 5.1). The image is in the public domain, but we obtained it from a hybrid investigative journalism/tabloid website called *The Smoking Gun*, which uses Freedom of Information Act requests to track down and publish legal documents, criminal records, court proceedings, and mug shots of various figures in the public eye. *The Smoking Gun* guarantees that everything on the site is "100% authentic," and its description of the "arresting images" that it publishes reinforces our point in Chapter 4 about the relationship between visual images and the construction of authenticity:

> While the artistry of photographers like RichardAvedon, Annie Leibovitz, and Yousuf Karsh provides the images of the powerful that will go down in history, TSG actually prefers the work of some more obscure shutterbugs. We're talking about the countless clerks, cops, and sheriff's

deputies who handle the impromptu photo shoots with the rich and famous who've landed in the pokey. Without the aid of fancy lighting, makeup, and wardrobe, these little works of mug shot art—taken with Instamatic, Polaroid, and digital cameras at law enforcement agencies nationwide—are perhaps the most candid photos of celebrities (and other public figures) that you'll see.

(*The Smoking Gun* 2008)

The website may have a point about the authenticity surrounding mug shots, because they are not produced primarily for media effect. But mug shots are close cousins of another kind of image produced by law enforcement agencies for what can only be described as dramatic reasons—the business celebrity "perp walk." The term describes the practice of parading alleged corporate perpetrators in handcuffs before the media after their arrest, and they became a staple of the business news media with the onset of the wave of post-dot.com era corporate scandals. "Once largely reserved for notoriously violent crimes that threatened the safety and security of the community, the perp walk has been extended to indicted chief executive officers and other corporate executives," noted an article in the *National Law Review* that provided advice on how executives might avoid the humiliation. "Indeed, whether for a law enforcement purpose or less laudable objectives of gaining advantage or inflicting intimidation, it now is common for white-collar defendants to be placed in what one federal appeals court has described as 'a posture connoting guilt'" (Mitchelson and Calloway 2006: S1).

Once mug shots or perp walk photos of fallen business celebrities get distributed, published in magazines, and plastered up on websites around the world, they become stock elements of an elaborately staged and ritualized media narrative. Media consumers schooled in the business celebrity eye, as we termed it in the last chapter, are familiar with such visual clichés even before they appear, which explains how the 2002 *BusinessWeek* cover image managed to visually invoke Kozlowski's mug shot a full three years before it was taken. For this reason it is not possible for *BusinessWeek* to use such a cover image to portray itself merely as a responsible muckraker exposing the "real" Kozlowski. As the magazine itself had to admit in the article behind the cover image, it had participated enthusiastically in the construction of Kozlowski's celebrity status in the first place. The mask in the illustration resembles any number of glowingly positive images of Kozlowski that *BusinessWeek* had been more than happy to promote in better times, including another cover photograph just seven months earlier celebrating Kozlowski as

"The Most Aggressive CEO" (BusinessWeek 2001). On one level, then, the image presumes to illustrate the unmasking of the real Kozlowski as a criminal, and the exposure of his former, idealized self as a fabrication and a lie. But on second glance it functions to expose the equally constructed and fragile nature of this new "truth," which, after all, consists of a digitally staged and doctored photograph.

Regardless of such glaring evidence of the media's own complicity in pumping up CEOs and turning them into celebrities in the first place, only to relish in their downfall later, in the midst of the backlash of 2002 the taint of scandal suddenly had convinced many that even happily married and law-abiding CEOs had never been worth their weight in stock options in the first place. "Over the past decade we've inflated the myth of the savior CEO, the chest-beating action figure who could single-handedly save or sink billion-dollar organizations," wrote *Fortune* contributing editor Jerry Useem. "The notion was mostly a crock—in truth, a company's fate depends on everything from market trends to an organization's history to pure luck" (Useem 2002). The note of conviction with which Useem delivered this verdict exemplified the manner in which so many sources characterized the backlash as the product of clear thinking and unclouded judgment, while painting the heedless enthusiasm for messianic management gurus and hero CEOs that came earlier as a "crock," a grievous collective mistake brought about by faulty logic and blinding cultural misconceptions.

An academic study by Harvard Business School researcher Rakesh Khurana published in 2002, and given widespread exposure in the news media throughout this period, bolstered such convictions. In *Searching for a Corporate Saviour: The Irrational Quest for Charismatic CEOs*, Khurana dissected the basic mechanics of the CEO labour market as it had developed over the last twenty years, paying particular attention to the influence of the cult of the celebrity CEO and to the reasons why large corporations came to look almost exclusively to external candidates to assume the reins of control and to serve as "corporate saviours" (Khurana 2002a). Khurana attributed these shifts not to the intrinsic benefits of the external CEO market in identifying potential leaders, but rather to a broader, historical transformation from managerial to investor-based capitalism, and to changes in American cultural understandings of the role of the CEO that accompanied that shift. According to Khurana, these structural and cultural factors resulted in the closing off of the outsider CEO market from any real competition, and to the limiting of the pool of potential new CEO candidates to a very small and homogeneous social group. "This process not only frequently fails to hire the best people available for the jobs at hand," observed Khurana, "but also tends to produce leaders with almost identical social, cultural, and demographic characteristics" (2002a: 108).

Khurana explained further that this situation had resulted in large part from the increasing size and visibility of institutional investors, and from their increasingly aggressive role in making management decisions on behalf of the companies in which they invest. As institutional investors came to own greater and greater portions of large companies stocks, they became less and less able to sell their shares when those companies underperformed. Left with no alternative, institutional investors began to intervene in the traditionally "cozy" relationship CEOs enjoyed with their boards, even to the point of demanding CEO resignations when companies failed to produce immediate results. This created incentives for boards to seek out new CEOs with as much star power and media appeal as possible, and to conceal the process of CEO selection from public view in order to safeguard against the perception that the selection process was somehow flawed. But flawed it was, argues Khurana, because it restricted CEO searches to a very small pool of potential candidates, and because it emphasized vague and elusive aspects of these candidates' personalities, such as "leadership" and "charisma." Undergirding this whole process, Khurana stressed, was "the fervent though erroneous belief that the quality of the CEO is the primary determinant of firm performance—and therefore that it is realistic to hope that a high-powered CEO can be a corporate saviour" (2002a: xiii). "Today's extraordinary trust in power of the charismatic CEO resembles less a mature faith than it does a belief in magic," said Khurana. "There is no conclusive evidence that a company's top leadership actually has much impact on its performance at all" (Khurana 2002b). These many inadequacies of the CEO labor market had contributed directly to the many corporate scandals that surfaced during this period, Khurana maintained, and had helped precipitate a severe crisis of leadership in corporate America.

At the root of Khurana's argument was a compelling case for the notion that the external CEO market is a social construction. In his words, "actors' perceptions of the market and of the structural position of actors in it are important constitutive dimensions of that market" (2002a: 43). The net effect of this argument was to challenge positivistic economic conceptions of markets and how they function in a manner that punctured the orthodox, agency-theory inspired justification for exorbitant CEO compensation and severance package. But Khurana went further, insisting that the CEO labour market was "merely an illusion, since the process of social construction consists precisely in making an institution look like an objective and external aspect of the environment." By characterizing the external CEO market as *merely* a social construction, and therefore inferior to some idealized notion of a market free of cultural preconceptions and social pressures, he raises the question of what such a non-socially constructed market would resemble. Like the many media sources that participated in the CEO celebrity backlash of the immediate post-New Economy period, then, Khurana implied heavily that his criticism of top management figures occupied a privileged, value-neutral vantage point outside of the influence of cultural and social dynamics.

Whether advanced in academic or media terms, such a position is untenable. Even if all the scandalous charges made against celebrity CEOs during this period were verifiably true (and many no doubt were), the enthusiasm and *schadenfreude* with which they were delivered would still call for a critical analysis of the historical and ideological roots of such an abrupt, cultural about-face. And this analysis would have to acknowledge that such waves of criticism themselves constitute a cultural phenomenon, because the celebrity CEO backlash of 2002 was by no means an isolated event. Although the business news media made much of the unprecedented nature of the onslaught at the end of the dot.com boom, it had happened before, several times over. As recently as December 2000, for example, *BusinessWeek* had criticized severely the urge to place the chief executive in a place of prominence in an article about what it called "The CEO Trap" (Bianco *et al.* 2000). Nearly a year before that, the *Wall Street Journal* had characterized the moment as a down cycle for American CEOs tantamount to "the twilight of the gods." The article had made much of a new breed of CEOs who had made a conscious decision to shun the limelight in order to focus instead on their companies' core businesses. "It's a different gang," said lawyer Ira Millstein in the article. "You're not going to see those heroic figures. It's a much more businesslike group of CEOs, maybe less glamorous as far as the public is concerned, but I hope just as good as the guys who came before them" (Pollock 1999: A1). Three years earlier, *Across the Board* actually had coined the term "backlash" to describe what it saw as a climate of recrimination against high-profile top executives. "The press has its knives sharpened for big business and its bosses," the magazine had noted. "Why aren't CEOs defending themselves?" (DePree and Mahoney 1996: 24).

Upon closer investigation, in fact, the media appear constantly in the process of discovering that the tides have turned against celebrity CEOs and business leaders, even up to the present day (Weidner 2008). When we take a longer view, the backlash itself turns out to form part of the staple diet of the business news media, a standardized trope or narrative device that gets trotted out again and again by successive generations of reporters and commentators, often with the validation of legal and academic experts. Every few years, it seems, the business news media announce the end of the era of the proverbial "Men in Black," the aggressive and rakish CEOs (both men and women, actually) upon whom they had previously showered so much attention, and trumpet instead the virtues of the "Men in Brown," who, ironically, get celebrated in the media for shunning the media limelight in order to concentrate on the bottom line. From this perspective, the backlash against CEO celebrities begins to look like just as much of a social construction as the phenomenon of CEO celebrity itself. The cyclical nature of the backlash against business celebrities, and the insistence of backlash enthusiasts that finally we have peeled back the layers of artifice and "constructedness" to get at the real truth about celebrity business figures, are more than vaguely reminiscent of some of the central characteristics of the kinds of management fashions we discussed in Chapter 3. In the next section of this chapter, therefore, we will draw out some of the connections between these two phenomena.

Don't be the last one on your block to knock business celebrities

As discussed in Chapter 3, academic theories about management fashions seek to describe the way that companies and consulting firms seem more and more eager to adopt and hype every next organizational improvement program, and then drop it for yet another one without any real sense of follow-through. It is important to remember that the management fashion perspective does not seek to dismiss such programs and techniques as nothing more than false beliefs, nor does the term "fashion" need to imply that such beliefs are merely ephemeral and therefore insignificant phenomenon. But such a dismissive critique of management fashions is built into the fashion phenomenon itself, and for this reason the fashion perspective can help us understand radical and often rapid cognitive shifts in central ideas and ideals about management techniques and management leaders. The focus in the management fashion literature on explaining these shifts renders the fashion perspective useful for exploring the seemingly overnight transformation from CEO celebration to CEO character assassination that we have observed taking place as a result of the backlash. From this vantage point, the business celebrity backlash is at once a rhetorical trope or narrative device that is mobilized to either shore up or tear down particular management fashions, and a minor management fashion in its own right.

To recall Abrahamson's definition, management fashions consist of generally accepted yet transitory beliefs, promoted by a community of management fashion setters, that certain techniques or practices lead to rational management progress. Abrahamson's emphasis on the management fashion setting community—a group roughly analogous to those we have called business culture intermediaries—reflects his institutional focus on the industry that produces management fashions, rather than simply on individual management techniques that rise and fall in popularity. In this book we have replicated this choice of focus with respect to business celebrities and the industries that produce them. Of particular relevance for our discussion of the business celebrity backlash is the emphasis in the management fashion literature on transitoriness. This emphasis carries with it the implication that one of the defining characteristics of any individual management fashion does not inhere to the theory or technique itself—it derives rather from the constant churn from one popular managerial fix to another. In fact the reasons for the churn may have nothing to do with the content of the fashion itself. As Abrahamson explains, management fashions must measure up to generally accepted social norms of rationality in order for the management community to accept them. But if these norms remain static for too long, progress will not appear to occur.

Abrahamson's emphasis on norms of rationality and progress helps explain one of the many curious things about management fashions. That is, no one involved in promoting them has much of an interest in advertising or even admitting the fleeting nature of their efforts, or of what those efforts may produce. Management fashions do not embrace their status as fashion. Rather, new (or recycled) management theories and techniques use a variety of rhetorical devices to dismiss other, previous theories and techniques as *mere* fashion, and to proclaim their own legitimacy as an innovation that looks *beyond the hype* to the *essence of management*, to paraphrase the title of Robert Eccles and Nitin Nohria's book about management fashions (Eccles and Nohria 1994). Behind the repeated insistence that this or that technique "is not just another management fashion" lies the not-so-subtle implication that previously accepted techniques were just that, and they no longer live up to norms of rational management progress. We might call this the "that was then, this is now" phenomenon, according to which all management fashions incorporate within their governing logic some element of backlash against previous fashions and techniques.

The emphasis on the connection between management fashions and norms of rationality and progress at the heart of Abrahamson's institutional perspective has drawn criticism from other scholars for being too narrow. Kieser, for example, argues for an expanded understanding of the many ways in which people relate to and make use of management fashions. In his perspective, "A management fashion is conceptualized as forming an arena in which different groups of participants bustle about—consultants, professors, managers, editors of management magazines, publishers, commercial seminar organizers, organizers of internet forums, etc" (Kieser 1997: 57). These various stakeholders, if we can call them that, can have a variety of different concerns and agendas. Some may be less concerned with creating the appearance of rational management progress than with satisfying emotional needs, others with shoring up political influence, or with simply making money. As Kieser explains it, "The participants can achieve their individual goals of highest possible profit, public image, power or career by widening the arena through luring further participants into it" (Kieser 1997: 57). Kieser's perspective is reinforced by the work of Tony Watson, who has discussed how management fashions can serve as a platform for a variety of different, even competing discourses, and can fulfill a variety of different organizational and individual needs aside from those for which they are ostensibly intended (Watson 1994).

All the characteristics of management fashions that we have highlighted in this section find their parallel in the phenomenon of business celebrity. Like management fashions, business celebrities are produced and defined by a number of actors and influences. Just as management fashions are distinguished as such primarily by their transitory nature rather than by their contents, so the status of a celebrity as celebrity is not intrinsic to the characteristics or personality of individual in question. It arises rather from the dynamics of the process of celebrification, and from the many social actors who participate in that process. Moreover, the process of celebrification is not just about building up business celebrities. It incorporates a cycle of rising and falling popularity, a churn of ever new and improved business celebrities, who often seem more than vaguely similar to those who came before. The same business culture intermediaries who help construct new business celebrities are often responsible for tearing down the old ones. As with the management fashion cycle, an element of backlash is hard-wired into the process of celebrification.

This is partly why the term celebrity itself often carries with it negative connotations. While many business culture intermediaries participate in the attribution of celebrity to this or that business figure, it would seem odd, and out of place, for such a figure to advance their own claims to celebrity status too overtly. Of course, Donald Trump is a glaring exception to this rule. "What is it about me that gets Larry King his highest ratings?" asks Trump himself in his trademark self-congratulatory manner. "When sweeps week comes I get a call from every television personality begging me to be on their show" (O'Brien 2005: 4). But most business luminaries at least pretend to reject media publicity—even as they pose for yet another magazine cover or grant another interview—in favor of something like "getting the job done," "focusing on their core business," or "increasing shareholder value." The reason for this has to do with the element of self-criticizing backlash built into the celebrity phenomenon itself, and with the strong connection between the popularity of a given type of business celebrity and the dominant contemporary norms of rationality and progress. With this in mind we might paraphrase Abrahamson's definition and describe the phenomenon of business celebrity as the collective, transitory belief, promoted by a community of business culture intermediaries, that certain individuals exemplify rational management progress.

As suggested by Keiser's critique of Abrahamson, and by our own model of business celebrity, the problem with this otherwise useful definition is that it does not account for the many different interests and agendas that are folded into the phenomenon of business celebrity. The arena thesis can help to connect a narrower, institutionalist understanding of the workings of the celebrity process to a broader, social perspective on what is at stake in that process. Keiser's suggestion that management fashions function as a sort of arena where these various parties bustle about and pursue their interests parallels our view of business celebrities as sites of debate and even conflict over what it means to be an individual in a complex, modern society dominated by business institutions, and over how it is possible for an individual to take action or to make a difference in the face of vast commercial, corporate, and social forces beyond their control.

Like management fashion, business celebrity is indeed a crass, commercial enterprise, and many of those who enter the business celebrity arena do so to pursue their own self-interest or simply to turn a quick buck. But to dismiss the phenomenon of business celebrity on these grounds is to ignore the broader cultural and ideological interests that also jostle for position within the arena of business celebrity. From this perspective the backlash against business celebrities is not merely a mechanism to keep the system functioning smoothly. Even the dismissal of the celebrity phenomenon by means of the backlash performs deeper ideological functions. In the remainder of this chapter we will examine more closely the ideological function of the business celebrity backlash, first by looking to the work of cultural studies scholars who have theorized about the role of anti-celebrity sentiments in a society so rife with enthusiasm for all things celebrity. Finally we will look at the ideology of anti-managerialism, which in various forms has mounted a sustained assault on the leaders of corporate enterprise ever since the rise of the large corporation itself.

Theorizing the backlash in cultural studies

Several of the cultural studies theorists whose work we discussed in Chapter 2 have sought to explain why the celebrity phenomenon can generate equal parts adoration and antagonism, devotion and disdain. We have referred to the work of Daniel Boorstin several times already in this book because his argument that celebrities are primarily famous for being famous is the most well-known and often-repeated piece of cultural analysis of celebrity to date. But Boorstin actually exemplifies the manner in which many cultural critics have not so much analyzed the backlash against celebrities built into the celebrity phenomenon as they have participated vigorously in the denouncing of celebrity as a false and vacuous form of cultural value. As Turner points out, "Boorstin's account was enclosed within a critique that accused contemporary American culture of a fundamental inauthenticity, as it was increasingly dominated by the media's presentation of what he calls the 'pseudo event'" (Turner 2004: 5). Gamson details how this form of critique has often dominated intellectual discussions of celebrity, especially when the news media try to report on how academics approach the topic (Gamson 1994: 9). According to Turner, this form of elite critique can provide only a limited insight into the dynamics of popular culture, because it indicts the direction in which that culture is developing as a matter of principle, seizing on the shifting fashions for this or that cultural phenomenon as proof of the charges. "Each new shift in fashion is offered as the end of civilization as we know it, with the real motivation being an elitist distaste for the demotic or populist dimension of mass cultural practices," he points out (Turner 2004: 5).

As mentioned in Chapter 2, however, not all theorists of cultural studies buy into this sort of manipulation thesis whereby audiences are duped by the power of the media into believing what are essentially portrayed as falsehoods or cultural hoaxes on a grand scale. Gamson, for example, reads into the elitist intellectual backlash against celebrity culture the very kind of debate we have located within the phenomenon of business celebrity itself. "Celebrity culture is itself built on major American fault lines: simultaneous pulls on the parts of producers and audiences alike to celebrate individual distinction and the equality of all, to demonstrate that success is available to all and available only to the special, to instate and to undermine a meritocratic hierarchy, to embrace and attack authority" (Gamson 1994: 12). From this perspective the swings over time from the adulation of celebrity figures to their denigration and back again begin to look like a debate over the value of celebrity itself, over what celebrities signify, and over how adequately they represent the culture of their time or the people who inhabit it. "In one sense, the celebrity represents success and achievement within the social world," notes Marshall. By granting a public stage to certain individuals, he says, the celebrity system recognizes and celebrates their importance. But Marshall is quick to point out that cultural attitudes towards celebrity are not coherent or ideologically consistent. "In another sense, the celebrity is viewed in the most antipathetic manner," he continues. "The sign of the celebrity is ridiculed and derided because it represents the center of false value. The success expressed in the celebrity posture is seen as success without the requisite association with work" (Marshall 1997: xi). From this perspective, he explains, celebrities are mere fabrications, which is why Boorstin described them as nothing more than pure images. "The celebrity sign is pure exchange value cleaved from use value," says Marshall, adopting the language of Marxist cultural critique to characterize this viewpoint. "It articulates the individual as commodity" (Marshall 1997: xi).

Despite the fact that the very word "celebrity" builds upon the notion of celebration, then, it has also come to carry with it what Marshall calls "an air of inauthenticity" and a certain "vulgar sense of notoriety" (Marshall 1997: 5). Even more so than these other theorists, Steven Connor places this negative connotation at the center of the celebrity phenomenon, and his explanation for the never-ending phenomenon of the celebrity backlash deserves a full discussion here. "Celebrities and celebrity are not accidentally at risk from shaming, debasement, defilement, and ritual humiliation," Connor argues. "It is the destiny and function of the celebrity to be exposed to scandal and absurdity and to bear its mark for ever" (Connor 2005: 5, 13). Connor interprets the kinds of recurrent bouts of celebrity backlash we have discussed in this chapter as proof that "the contemporary culture of celebrity is intricately and intrinsically threaded through with envy, hostility, fear and rage" (Connor 2005: 4). Celebrities exist to be exposed, he says, both in the sense of being made visible to the widest possible audience and in the sense of being stripped naked or revealed. The point of this latter kind of exposure for Connor is not to uncover the celebrities for what they really are, but rather to fulfill an almost ritual need for public displays of antipathy and degradation in a society characterized by gross imbalances of power. Rojek, who emphasizes the quasi-religious or liminal functions of celebrity, describes such rituals as ceremonies of mortification, which function to bring the heavenly body of the celebrity back down to earth (Rojek 2001: 80).

From the perspective developed by Marshall, which emphasizes how celebrities embody affective power, Connor's contribution is to illuminate the dark underside of the affects and emotions to which celebrity power can give rise. Connor's argument rests on the distinction he draws between celebrity, on the one hand, and fame or renown on the other. For him these latter two terms connote notoriety or sheer visibility, but do not involve the dynamics of celebration, charisma, or emotion that celebrity entails. He explains:

> For me to acknowledge a public figure as a celebrity is to assent to the fact that they are the object of celebration. The celebrity is not just well-known, they are in-celebration, to-be-celebrated. To have fame means to be famous, the noun and the adjective closing together like the pages of a book. Fame is fate: celebrity is being fêted. To be a celebrity is to stand in present need of celebration.
>
> (Connor 2005: 6)

What is important for Connor in this distinction is that the phenomenon of celebrity demands the active emotional participation of the audience, including the celebration of the fact of celebrity itself. In making this argument, Connor helps to clarify how celebrities can wield the power to instill in media audiences the kind of abstract desire Marshall describes. As Connor explains it:

> The celebrity is the also bearer of the power that, since the late nineteenth-century, has been generated in abundance by the apparatus of mass communication, namely the power of fascination. This is not simply the power to mesmerize, captivate or enchant. This is to say that the power does not simply flow (as in popular fantasies of "influence") unidirectionally from the fascinator to his or her subjects. In fact, the dream scheme of celebrity involves complicated circulations of powers, in which agency and passivity undergo strange reversals and convolutions. The fascinator's power is the power to awaken in the subject of enchantment the desire to be subjected to power.
>
> (Connor 2005: 7)

In Connor's view, then, the celebrity's power to fascinate consists of an ability to awaken in the audience the kind of abstract desire Marshall describes. But Connor goes on to argue that the power to awaken this kind of enchantment comes at a significant cost, because it can generate considerable resentment on the part of media audiences at being placed in a position of subjugation. At the root of the ambivalence baked into the celebrity phenomenon, Connor argues, is "our resentment of their presumption in soliciting acknowledgement of their celebrity" (Connor 2005: 6). The most obvious indicator of this resentment, he points out, is the dismissal of the lower ranks of celebrities as unworthy of such acknowledgment and admiration. "Because the condition of celebrity always involves presumption or demand, we feel entitled to deride those who claim to be celebrities without our ever having heard of them, even though the oxymoronic category of Unknown Celebrity is swelling all the time" (Connor 2005: 6).

In extreme cases, the resentment that celebrity generates can lead to outbursts of fan violence. But according to Connor the ritual of degradation via the media at the heart of the celebrity backlash phenomenon is a more effective means of achieving the same end, because the celebrity remains available for more abuse later. Besides, Connor remarks, it is not the living, breathing individual that generates the resentment, but rather the fictional creature that we call a celebrity. "Even if their hurt is gratifyingly larger than life, celebrities, like toys or cartoon characters, cannot be hurt because it is well known that they don't exist," Connor observes. "Besides which, they always deserve the ridicule they attract, because of the power we think they think they have over us" (Connor 2005: 13). For these reasons Connor argues that the production of celebrity takes place specifically for the purposes of allowing for this kind of defilement. In other words, the backlash is the foundation of the phenomenon of celebrity itself. As Connor concludes, "what we really want is for them always to be there, at once adored and detested, our adoration the alibi for the vileness we require them to carry, and the defilement they must suffer the brake on our excessive adoration" (Connor 2005: 13).

The CEO celebrity backlash and the cultural politics of antimanagerialism

Connor's is an extreme view, and it may seem odd to apply words like defilement and degradation to the treatment of business figures in the media. But, as made clear throughout this chapter, there does seem to be an almost ritual aspect to the business celebrity backlash. The significance of that ritual derives not only from the institutional dynamics of the celebrity industries, nor merely from media audience responses to the presumption of those industries, but also from the broader cultural and institutional context of corporate capitalism in which the celebrity and media industries thrive. In the end, this constant back and forth about the virtues of this or that business celebrity, and about the value of the phenomenon of business celebrity itself, constitutes a debate about who should run some of the most powerful institutions in contemporary society. And in the context of this broader debate, the backlash reflects the influence of a loosely connected set of ideas and arguments which we might define under the umbrella of the terms managerialism and anti-managerialism.

In a general sense, managerialism refers to a belief in the efficiency of management and the advisability of handing over the control of public and private institutions to professional managers. As Tony Watson explains, the word has come to define "approaches to public administration or government in which most problems are seen as soluble by managerial means—are seen, in effect, as administratively technical matters rather than as political, ideological or value matters" (Watson 2003: 248). But managerialism also has a more specific origin and meaning in relation to American legal theories about the nature and function of the corporation. In this context the term refers to an ideology that arose in the late nineteenth and early twentieth centuries to legitimize the organizational development of the large corporation and the strata of top executives who controlled them.

As noted in Chapter 1, the rise of big business in the United States challenged previously dominant conceptions of the individual and of individual agency, shaking the roots of the kind of liberal ideology that viewed the marketplace as the forum where free, propertied individuals came to trade goods, services, products, and ideas. In their landmark 1932 book, *The Modern Corporation and Private Property*, Adolf Berle and Gardiner Means advanced what has come to be called the managerialist thesis, which gave these concerns a specific articulation and legal rationale. According to Berle and Means, the rightful owners of large business institutions were their shareholders, but such institutions had become so big that shareholders could no longer maintain meaningful control of them. That control had fallen by default into the hands of a professionalized managerial bureaucracy that was supposed to act on behalf of the owners, but that did not necessarily have the interests of the shareholders in mind. More importantly, Berle and Means feared, managers did not have the interests of the general public in mind, so that the most powerful institutions in society could not be expected to act automatically in the public's best interests. "Berle and Means thus wrote of a small group, sitting at the head of enormous organizations, with the power to build, and destroy, communities, to generate great productivity and wealth, but also to control the distribution of that wealth, without regard for those who elected them (the stockholders) or those who depended on them (the larger public)," explains Mark Mizruchi in a recent reassessment of the managerialist thesis. "This was hardly a cause for celebration, and Berle and Means, in the tradition of Thomas Jefferson, expressed considerable concern about this development" (Mizruchi 2004: 581).

In a certain sense, one might argue, Berle and Means were the first anti-managerialists, since they were not at all happy with the position corporate managers had come to enjoy. But they also pointed towards a way out of the dilemma they defined, and in so doing exemplified how a corporate liberal version of managerialism would help reconcile corporate managerial power with liberal democratic ideals. "Indeed, it seems almost essential if the corporate system is to survive," they insisted, "that the 'control' of the great corporations should develop into a purely neutral technocracy, balancing a variety of claims by various groups in the community and assigning to each a portion of the income stream on the basis of public policy rather than private cupidity" (Berle and Means 1967: 312). Corporate liberal managerialism resolved the contradictions between concentrated economic power and democratic interests by means of the application of technocratic, psychological, bureaucratic, and managerial expertise. As historian James Livingston has pointed out, adherents to corporate liberalism argued that the rise of corporate power represented "not the end but the renewal of individual opportunity and social mobility for the American middle classes old and new," because "within the new corporate bureaucracies, the determinants of status were to be natural talents, past effort, and learned skills, not familial connections or inherited wealth" (1992: 31).

The cultural politics of anti-managerialism are convoluted and contradictory, especially when one considers its relationship to high-profile business celebrities. On the one hand, the backlash against business celebrities can be seen to tarnish the reputation of all top managers, and to call into question the idea of ever handing over corporate control to such runaway figures. Images of ne'er-do-well CEOs in handcuffs or behind bars certainly can function to make all CEOs look bad. From this perspective the business celebrity backlash stems from an anti-managerialist impulse to contain such personal concentrations of power and prerogative, and to knock the top strata of the managerial class off their pedestal. On the other hand, we might interpret the backlash as an extension of managerialist concerns that commercial institutions should serve the interests of their shareholders, and perhaps also the interests of the public at large, but certainly not just the interests of a small stratum of very powerful top executives. During the ouster of Carly Fiorina as CEO of Hewlett Packard in 2005, for example, many sources condemned Fiorina for being more concerned about her own celebrity stature than about the health of the company or the value of its shares. Fiorina's successor Mark Hurd was touted as one of the "Men in Brown" who would not try to draw so much attention to himself (Guthey and Jackson 2008). From this perspective the CEO celebrity backlash serves a legitimizing function, isolating celebrity CEO malefactors as bad apples that need to be sorted out so that the managerialist system can continue to function smoothly.

From yet another perspective, charismatic celebrity business figures embody an anti-managerialist critique of management bureaucracies and the stifling lock they maintain on creativity, innovation, and entrepreneurial energy. Co-author Eric Guthey has written a series of articles on how such figures as CNN founder Ted Turner and Netscape entrepreneur Jim Clark came to function in the popular business media as anti-managerial business celebrities. Although his star has largely faded now, for example, Ted Turner enjoyed nearly a decade as the pre-eminent bad boy of American business. Dubbed "Captain Outrageous" and "Terrible Ted," he originally came to prominence as much for his rakish demeanor and swashbuckling sailing exploits in the America's Cup as he did for his business acumen. But in a manner typical of the celebrification process as we have described it, the media never managed to maintain clear-cut boundaries between Turner's personal life and business endeavors, and always sought to use Turner's colorful gaffes and private excesses to spice up the otherwise dreary news on the business pages. Even Turner's marriage and sex-life with actress Jane Fonda became a prism through which to understand the business zeitgeist. As Guthey has argued, his much celebrated personal biography became nearly indistinguishable from a narrative about a particular era in the development and deregulation of the media industries, not only in the USA but globally as well. In this manner Turner became the premier icon of a new ideological construct Guthey has called "corporate neo-liberalism":

> His symbolic effect has been to supplant the bureaucratic rationality of corporate liberalism with market efficiencies, its technical expertise with an "aw- shucks" enthusiasm for satellite gadgetry, and its paternalistic

trusteeship with the virtues of youthful and regenerative entrepreneurship. In this regard he embodies the market exuberance we associate with the new economic theory of the firm, and this is why he has never legitimized corporate media management in the top-down, paternalistic mode of a Thomas Edison, a David Sarnoff, or a William Paley. No matter how gray-haired Turner gets, he maintains a youthful, rebellious, seductive and boyish aura of naïveté and acquisitiveness . . . Rather than separate ownership from control, or do away with both, Turner combines both ownership and control back together again in his own person, presenting himself as a new, tangible, anti-bureaucratic and competitive-masculine embodiment of corporate leadership and responsibility.

(Guthey 2001: 131)

Netscape's Jim Clark, meanwhile, was portrayed in star business journalist Michael Lewis's book *The New New Thing* as a "Disorganization Man" so allergic to large, gray, corporate bureaucracies that he was constantly trying to design companies that would have no room for Jim Clark in them. As Lewis described it, Clark's every encounter with "the American professional management class" convinced him that there is "a whole layer of people in American business who called themselves managers who were in fact designed to screw up his plans" (Lewis 2000: 63). Guthey has argued that the difference in media portrayals of Turner and Clark pointed towards an intensification of the anti-managerial strain in the popular culture of corporate capitalism, and towards the predominance in the years surrounding the millennium of an ethos of what he calls "New Economy Romanticism." As he has explained:

Ted Turner's brand of antimanagerialism argued that corporations could best fulfill their public interest obligations not by the regulatory imposition of managerial trusteeship, but rather by the expansion of consumer choice, in his case made possible by cable and broadcast deregulation. But notions of corporate responsibility and the public interest don't even appear on Jim Clark's radar screen. He strikes anti-corporate postures without even recognizing the corporate threat to meaningful participation in the democratic polity. For Clark, the corporation is simply a drag, because it prevents him from enjoying the abundance of material goods and entrepreneurial opportunities made possible by the Internet. In this manner New Economy Romanticism completes the task of erasing citizenship and elevating consumption as the vital core of what it means to be a person in a corporate society. As a social type, Clark exhibits all the characteristics of the ultimate consumer: a restless addiction to accumulation for its own sake; a short attention span for each latest acquisition; a preference for immediate self-gratification over commitment to sustainable institutions; and a narcissistic obsession with keeping ahead of the Joneses—or Bill Gateses, or Larry Ellisons.

(Guthey 2004: 329)

The CEO celebrity backlash of 2002 brought the era of New Economy Romanticism to an abrupt end, but the ever shifting cycles of celebrification continue to churn up and recycle elements of New Economy rhetoric in new contexts in connection with new business figures. As we have argued in this chapter, these constant back-and-forth shifts point towards a pervasive and inescapable cultural ambivalence over the power that certain individuals can gain by rising to the top of business institutions, and over the influence that large corporations exert over modern society. The backlash reaction against business celebrities exemplifies the manner in which such figures can function as flashpoints for debates and conflicts over what business leadership should be like, and over what it means to be a person in a society dominated by business institutions. As we discuss in the next chapter, the complex cultural and ideological dynamics of business celebrity bashing exert considerable influence over discussions about what leadership is, and about who should rightfully exercise it. As we argue, it is especially important to understand these complex dynamics as leadership itself has become increasingly celebrified, and as scholarly research on leadership has launched its own backlash against the celebrified figure of the heroic leader.

6   The celebrification of heroic leadership

Imagine yourself stomping into Jack Welch's office and demanding his secrets for dynamic leadership: or, marching into Andy Grove's office for a discourse on management theory; or, slipping into Carl Icahn's office and soliciting his ideas on finance. Why stomp, march and slip? Because it is unlikely we will be invited. Of course, if we were to invite ourselves in to their office, we would undoubtedly be escorted out by two burly security guards and the FBI would be running a background check on us within the hour. But just imagine having the opportunity to sit down not only with today's captains of industry, but yesterday's icons as well. What advice would Andrew Carnegie, John D. Rockefeller, and J. Paul Getty give us on leadership, management, finance, and other components essential to achieving success? The *Book of Business Wisdom* provides this enchanting opportunity.

(Krass 1997: 1)

This paragraph opens a book containing a collection of extracts of writing by fifty-four different business leaders, many of whom are no longer living, almost all of whom hailed from the United States. The editor of this collection exhorts his readers to admire and learn from these leaders. He closes his introduction by saying, "As you read the selections, allow these captains of industry to come alive in your mind; hear the vitality of their character; listen to their distinct voices and unique ideas; but, also search for and understand the common threads they share" (Krass 1997: xv). Such books are of course legion. They capitalize on the phenomenon of business celebrity even as they contribute to the process of celebrification itself. They also capitalize upon and contribute to a celebrified notion of leadership. In this chapter we will examine how the celebrification of business leaders contributes to the production of a particular set of discourses and practices of leadership.

The argument we have developed in this book about the construction of business celebrities opens up a new way to look at the phenomenon of leadership. From the conventional point of view, leadership is a natural human and social activity that is necessary for the proper functioning of all manner of organizations and institutions. But, from the perspective developed in this book, leadership, like celebrity, is the product of a set of overlapping industries. These industries are largely responsible for the fact that in recent years leadership has become something that everyone is encouraged to work on, to develop, and to study. Leadership development has become a major priority for politicians, business leaders, policy-makers, and educators the world over. Leadership is widely seen as both the problem and solution to all manner of contemporary issues: from ending world poverty to addressing global warming; from turning around ailing corporations to regenerating local communities; from reviving schools to creating scientific breakthroughs. In this chapter we will describe the centrally important role that business celebrities play in the rapidly growing, multi-billion dollar global "leadership industries."

We believe it is important to understand leadership as a product of the many organizational, promotional, and discursive practices that characterize the leadership industries. From this perspective, leadership is not merely an empirical object to be studied or a set of desirable characteristics to be developed or a collection of best practices to be disseminated by leadership scholars, trainers, coaches, or consultants. In fact, the diverse activities of these and many other actors and institutions all contribute in a direct and sub-stantive manner to the production of leadership itself, both as an intellectual concept and as a cultural commodity. This means that it is not strictly accu-rate to talk about "leadership" in the singular, because it consists of a variety of different products, services, and theoretical formulations.

It is hard to gauge the true scale and scope of the leadership industries, partly because they are so under-researched. Burgoyne (2004) has estimated that organizations spend between 36 and 60 billion US dollars annually on leadership development throughout the world, and this figure is certainly growing. John Storey (2004) accounts for this growth by pointing to four different types of salient explanation. The conventional explanation points to the increased complexity and rapid pace of contemporary society, which demand ever higher and more creative levels of leadership. The institutional explanation emphasizes the pressure that individuals and organizations feel to join the leadership bandwagon in order to maintain credibility and build their reputation. If everyone is doing leadership development, so the rationale goes, we'd better do it too. The sociological explanation highlights the role that leadership can play in legitimizing the authority, power, and privilege of elites. It provides a socially acceptable means of justifying the status quo. Finally, the strategic advantage explanation argues that leadership is an intangible asset that must be cultivated in order to gain a rare and valuable source of competitive advantage.

In this chapter we argue that the celebrification processes we have discussed in the previous five chapters play a major role in promoting an abstract desire to acquire leadership capabilities by consuming leadership products (Meindl *et al*. 1985). In a certain sense leadership itself has become a celebrity, and celebrity entrepreneurs, CEOs, and management gurus, along with the business culture intermediaries who produce them for public consumption, all serve to bolster the "celebrification" of leadership itself. In fact, we can readily trace the contribution that business celebrities make in all four types of explanation that John Storey has put forward to explain the widespread interest in leadership. Most obviously, celebrity entrepreneurs, CEOs, and management gurus provide powerful exemplars of individuals who have succeeded in an increasingly competitive environment because they are purported to have provided higher levels of and more creative forms of leadership. The accessible, engaging, and highly codified accounts of their success provide us with exemplars that can be readily emulated and followed. The widespread celebration of their success serves to normalize and legitimize the authority and power of elites. After all, don't they deserve what they have received, and won't I too have a shot at that if I learn from their fine example? Finally, the rare, mysterious, and elusive nature of leadership that is promulgated in accounts of celebrity entrepreneurs, CEOs, and management gurus serves to underline and reinforce leadership as the ultimate competitive advantage.

We will begin this chapter by showing that business celebrities have not only played a major role in promoting leadership, but they have been responsible for promoting a particular form of leadership. That is, a "heroic" form of leadership. This form of leadership suggests that leadership stems from singularly influential individuals who possess special qualities that mark them out to do great deeds by overcoming many obstacles. Burns (1978) suggests that heroic leadership is distinguished by a relationship between the leader and the led, in which belief in the leader is based on personage rather than experience or past performance. Heroic notions of leadership are nothing new. In fact, they can be traced back to Plato and Homer. Heroes have always acted as important role models of achievement to be emulated.

They serve both as figures of production as well as figures of consumption. Drawing on a sample of books that purport to draw out the leadership lessons that can be gleaned from studying business celebrity leadership books, we will show how these accounts seductively guide their readers to follow and embrace heroic models of leadership.

In the second part of the chapter we describe the critique of these heroic models of leadership which has gathered momentum, largely from academic commentators, but increasingly from the consultant community. This critique centers on the inappropriateness and non-tenability of these heroic models of leadership on moral, political, and instrumental grounds within the rapidly changing context of the post-industrial, knowledge-based era. In its stead, an emergent post-heroic model of leadership is presented that emphasizes the importance of a shared, distributed model of leadership. We will argue that these critiques have failed on two counts. First of all, they have failed to conduct a sufficiently close reading of the business celebrities themselves, and the things that they say and write. A closer reading would reveal not just one but a variety of "heroic leadership" models, many of which actively advocate and support the shared and distributed leadership models that are a feature of the alternative post-heroic leadership models. Second, because so many critics of heroic leadership focus their attention on the "business celebrity" *per se*, they ignore the interactive nature of the celebrification processes that have been stressed in this book. As we have made clear, there is a certain irony in the fact that the celebrification of these figures is not driven by a heroic top-down, hierarchic leadership model, but by a highly complex, distributed, and networked model system of leadership.

The chapter closes by discussing efforts to rehabilitate the heroic model of leadership in the face of the celebrity CEO backlash that we described in the previous chapter. In the face of the backlash, many scholars and authors have sought to champion an authentic and altruistic form of leadership that they believe liberates hero leaders from the celebrification processes we have described in this book. Authentic heroic approaches to leadership emphasize achievement, altruism, emulation, ethical judgment, and humility. They also earnestly reject commodification, mediation, and attribution. We will argue, however, that celebrification remains central to the successful promotion and adoption of even this rehabilitated form of humble heroic leadership, in spite of the fact that those who produce this kind of leadership product would deny this. Without celebrification, these enlightened models of heroic leadership would not have the power to challenge, inform, and engage the very practitioners they are targeting.

Heroic leaders as business celebrities

In Chapter 4, we referred to Andrzej Huczynski's pioneering book, *Management Gurus*, in which he set out to describe and explain the rise of a new wave of management ideas that he dubbed "guru theory." Huczynski identified three types of "guru" whom he argued were the main proponents of this body of theory: "academic gurus," such as Warren Bennis, Michael Porter, and Henry Mintzberg, who maintained their business school affiliation; "consultant gurus," such as Tom Peters, John Naisbitt, and Stephen Covey, who had academic backgrounds but had gone out on their own to set up their own consulting firms; and "hero managers" such as Lee Iaccoca (Chrysler), Victor Kiam (Remington), and Donald Trump, current or past CEOs who were widely acknowledged to have been successful and more than a little different in terms of their personality and somewhat unconventional in how they got things done. Referring back to the typology of business celebrities that we presented in the opening chapter we can see an obvious connection between our celebrity entrepreneurs and celebrity CEOs and Huczysnki's hero managers as well as a link between celebrity management gurus and Huczysnki's academic and consultant gurus.

"Hero manager" would seem to be an apt epithet. The *Oxford English Dictionary* states that the term "Hero" originated as a name given to men of superhuman strength, courage, or ability, who were favored by the Gods. Later notions of heroes included men of renown supposedly to be deified on account of great and noble deeds, from which they were also venerated generally or locally.

Thomas Carlyle, the man most closely associated with expounding a philosophy of heroism, argued that history was made by great men such as Mohammed, Shakespeare, and Cromwell, who appeared as the situation required and existed independently of their followers. In his book *On Heroes and Hero Worship*, he developed his thesis that people need a strong and ruthless ruler and should obey him (Carlyle 1910). Any philosophy of history which emphasized the importance of general causes seemed to him to imply a simple mechanical doctrine and to deny the efficacy of the great spiritual forces. Moreover, in advocating the benefits of "hero worship," Carlyle stated that "no sadder proof can be given by a man of his own littleness than disbelief in great men." By way of critical counterweight, his contemporary, Herbert Spencer, observed that "hero worship is strongest where there is least regard for human freedom." Friedrich Nietzsche, the other philosopher most closely associated with heroism, provided us with Superman, a human who appears in many guises and has battled modern values and overcome the flaws of humanity (Kaufman 1968). Rejecting the idea of God, Superman is a real individual who creates values that are firmly rooted in the everyday changing world. This is someone who, by trusting his own intuitive sense of what is good and evil, succeeds better than any other. Only by following his example can we hope to improve ourselves and our society. Thus was the blueprint for twentieth-century comic book heroes so intractably spun (Fingeroth 2004).

This heroic ideal can be traced through to autobiographical accounts or biographical accounts of business leaders which first came to prominence in the early part of the twentieth century. Indeed some of the foundational texts of management were written not by academics but by practicing managers. For example, Henry Fayol, a French mining engineer and manager who is widely credited with "inventing" management by distinguishing it as a separate activity and defining its constituent elements, drew on his lifelong experience of running the mining and metallurgical combine, Commentary-Fourchamboult-Decazeville (Fayol 1949). In *My Years with General Motors*, Alfred Sloan, the head of General Motors from the early 1920s to the mid-1950s, virtually invented the decentralized, multi-divisional corporation (Sloan 1963). Drawing on forty years with the Bell Telephone Company, Chester Barnard wrote *The Functions of the Executive*, a book which has exerted tremendous influence upon corporate life, and which argued, well before it became fashionable, that the role of the CEO was to manage the values of the organization and secure employee commitment (Barnard 1938).

In contrast to these more established books, the new breed of hero manager books that became a fixture of book stores from the early 1980s onward sell in considerably larger numbers to a much wider public. Their focus has also shifted away from establishing universal and timeless principles of management to explicating the personality and persona of the CEO. Henry Fayol, Alfred Sloan, and Chester Barnard do not figure prominently in their accounts. The corporation is the key concern. By contrast, accounts of Jack Welch, Richard Branson, and Bill Gates dwell on who they are, on how they got to where they are, and on how their philosophies of life got them there, in ways that touch on issues far beyond the confines of the boardroom. In this regard these contemporary hero manager accounts have more in common with their celebrity peers in other fields than the earlier hero manager accounts did. The following quote taken from the inside of a bookjacket is emblematic:

> Of all the outstanding business leaders of our time, none can boast the almost universal respect—awe, even—that Jack Welch receives from

colleagues and competitors alike. As the Chairman of General Electric, he has transformed the company into a Goliath of the new economy with his unique management style, forward-thinking approach, and inspiring leadership. *Welch: An American Icon* delivers a rare, behind-the-scenes look at how this man has become a global symbol of brilliant management, shedding new light on the tactics, style and personality of the man who made GE a dominating force.

(Lowe 2001)

Writing from the vantage point of the early 1990s, Huczysnki noted that, compared to academic and consultant gurus, hero manager gurus tend to be few and far between. Most managers prefer to keep a low profile, stay out of the limelight, and get on with what they do best. By the same token, many senior executives we have spoken to have at some point thought about and secretly harness a desire to write "that management book" if they could ever find the time. Those hero manager books that do take off invariably do so in quite spectacular fashion. However, hero managers are usually good for one book. For example, Lee Iaccocoa's autobiography impressively entitled *IACCOCA* was the number-one best-seller in the US in 1984 and 1985, selling well over 1 million copies in both years (Iaccoca and Novak 1985). The sequel to this book, *Talking Straight*, sold comparatively fewer copies and disappeared largely without trace (Iacocca and Kleinfeld 1988). Richard Branson appears to have had better luck with his sequel to *Losing My Virginity* (Branson 1999), graphically entitled *Screw It* (Branson 2006).

As we saw in Chapters 1 and 2, hero managers attract considerable media attention in the form of newspapers and magazine profiles either purposely or otherwise. This widespread and consistent interest eventually translates into a book about them written either by them or more generally ghost-written by a professional writer, usually a journalist. The hero managers write these books for a number of reasons. For example, in *Losing My Virginity*, Richard Branson explains, "having come close to dying over the Atlas Mountains, I thought I should write this book now, in case my guardian angel ever deserts me." He adds, "I have also written this book to show how we made Virgin what it is today. Rather like our balloon flights, these years have been all about survival. If you read carefully between the lines you will, I hope, understand our vision and where it is we are going" (Branson 1999). Another hero manager had more altruistic ends in mind. In *Body and Soul* (1991), Anita Roddick explains that, in writing the book, "What we are trying to do is to create a new business paradigm, simply by showing that business can have a human face and a social conscience." Indeed that book did much to publicize and popularize the corporate social responsibility movement which has now well and truly entered the mainstream of management thinking and popular discourse.

In Chapter 4 we noted that academic and consultant gurus work in a variety of media. While the crowded calendars of fully employed hero managers prevents them from exploiting the full range of media, those who are partially employed or retired can become staples of the celebrity speaker circuit; they are featured in videos and DVDs; and a number of them have gone on to host their own television shows, most notably John Harvey-Jones in *Troubleshooter*, Donald Trump in *The Apprentice*, and Alan Sugar in the UK version of *The Apprentice*. Academics and consultants have, however, in general proved to be more adept at inventing and repackaging their message. It is, after all, difficult for hero managers to reinvent the careers that are the basis of their leadership philosophy. During the 1990s, the heyday of management fashions and gurus, most gurus tended to fall into either the academic or consultant camps. In the early part of the twenty-first century, however, there has been a discernible trend in favor of hero managers. It is possible that business-book buyers have decided that they prefer to hear directly from those who have "gone out and done it," rather than those who have talked about it or studied it from afar. Why rely on an academic or a consultant to tell you what is going on either second- or third-hand when you can learn first-hand from a chief executive?

The leadership lessons of the business celebrity

In its July 28, 2003 issue *Fortune* magazine ran a cover story entitled "The 10 Greatest CEOs of All Time: Learn from Them." The author, Jim Collins, author of *Built to Last* (Collins and Porras 1994) and *Good to Great* (Collins 2001a), and a consultant guru in his own right, observed:

> For good reason, we've become cynical about CEOs. There seem to be no heroes left standing, no one to emulate or believe in. There's an increasingly gloomy sense that we should simply throw up our hands and give up on corporate leadership. I disagree. Having spent the last year studying what separates great companies from mediocre ones, I can say unequivocally: There are role models to learn from—albeit not the ones you might expect.

> (Collins 2003: 55)

In rank order the leaders that Jim Collins selected were Charles Coffin, who created General Electric Co.; Bill Allen who saved Boeing in the post-war period; Sam Walton, founder of Wal-Mart; Goerge Merck, former CEO of Merck & Co.; Darwin Smith, former CEO of Kimberly-Clark; James Burker, CEO of Johnson & Johnson; David Maxwell, CEO of Fannie Mae; William McKnight, CEO of 3M; Katherine Graham, CEO of Washington Post Co.; and David Packard, co-founder of Hewlett-Packard. In explaining the rationale for selecting and advocating these ten business leaders, Collins states: "If the question is how to identify more of the right leaders—and how a new generation can learn to *become* the right leaders—there is no better answer than these ten. In an age of diminished standards, those they set loom larger than ever" (Collins 2003: 56) Jim Collins' response to the "CEO backlash" described in Chapter 5 is not to question the celebrification of business leaders but to change his frame of reference from today's corporate scene to the past, in which context he argues that heroes were heroes, and *not* celebrities.

Jim Collins is not alone in looking nostalgically to a golden era of superlative corporate leadership. *Forbes* magazine which originated the "400 Richest Americans" special issue back in 1982, is in the vanguard of celebrating and rehabilitating corporate leaders from the past. In the foreword to the *Forbes Greatest Business Stories of All Time* (Gross 1996), Timothy Forbes, a grandson of B.C. Forbes, glowingly refers to his grandfather's book entitled, *Men Who Are Making America* (Forbes 1917). In addition to raising the capital required to launch *Forbes* magazine, the book established his reputation as "the human-izer of business" (Gross 1996: 2). In the foreword to a companion book, *Forbes Great Success Stories*, Steve Forbes, another grandson of B.C. Forbes, recalled that he used to say "You'd learn more about a business by sizing up the "head-knocker" (his word for CEO) than you would from the company's balance sheet" (Farnham 2000: viii).

The *Investor's Business Daily* runs a "leaders and success" section which features a short biographical sketch of a leader. Over the years spent analyzing leaders and successful people "in all walks of life," it has noted that most of these have ten traits that, when combined, "can turn dreams into reality." Each day the section highlights one of these ten by describing the life of a particular leader. These traits include: How you think is everything; Decide upon your true dream and goals: take action; Be persistent and work hard; Learn to analyze details; Focus your time and money; Don't be afraid to innovate; Be different; Deal and communicate with people effectively; Be honest and dependable; Take responsibility (*Investor's Business Daily* 2004).

Such has been the scale and interest in business leaders from the past that a new type of business book has emerged that seeks to provide a compendium of business leaders and thinkers. For example, *Fifty Key Figures in Management* identifies people "who, through their ideas or by practice and example, have made a major contribution to how management is understood and done" (Witzel 2003: xii). *Movers and Shakers: The People Behind Business Today* provides forty-five profiles of management thinkers, largely composed of academic and consultant gurus, and fifty-five profiles of "business giants" or hero managers (Bloomsbury Reference Book 2004). In producing the book, the authors note, "our aim has been to identify the key figures in a range of industries who by their efforts have transformed the way business is conducted. Being nice is not one of the main criteria; being effective is." In the Foreword to the book, Robert Heller notes that the largely ghost-written books about business giants "are not templates for management success but they can be spurs to encourage readers to search with equal alertness and vigor for the ground-floor opportunity into which they can pour their entire being" (2004: x). Summarizing how he believes managers and entrepreneurs can best learn from these business giants, Heller concludes: "This type of simplicity is generally the hallmark of the supreme mover and shaker, and of the greatest teachers. It makes it easier for readers to learn their lessons and to apply the management wisdom of a world-changing mind. What if, at first, you don't succeed like the giants, try, try, try again. And when you do succeed, still imitate them—try even harder" (2004: xii). The publishing industry has obviously seen an opportunity to tap into a nostalgic desire on the part of practicing managers who, tired of the excessive hype and the backlash that has been accorded to contemporary hero managers, now look to the past for inspirational hero managers who emerged during what is widely perceived to be the golden age of pre-business celebrity heroism. There is a certain degree of irony here in that many of these hero managers were, in fact, the original creations of the celebrity industry just as it was moving from its infancy to its adolescence.

The rise of the non-Anglo-American business celebrity

The ranks of hero managers, in common with their academic and consultant guru cousins, have consisted largely of white American males, along with a token handful of British-born managers. There are also many business books that celebrate business leaders of largely American extraction who have succeeded overseas. For example, *China CEO: Voices of Experience from 20 International Business Leaders* contains interviews with twenty top executives who head up operations in the "must-win" Chinese market. "International" in this context means "Westerners not from China" (Fernandez and Underwood 2006). There have been some notable exceptions to this general bias, that is, business leaders who have emerged from non-Anglo-American contexts and received worldwide attention. Perhaps the most well known of these is Ricardo Semler, a Brazilian manager for the manufacturing company Semco who attracted global attention with *Maverick* (Semler 1993). The book describes his revolutionary approach to management, which involved exchanging the organizational pyramid for a circle, throwing out managers and giving employees control over their jobs and their lives.

While relatively few CEOs attain global status, it has become common practice for country-specific publishers to produce books that celebrate the prowess and success of their own home-grown business leaders. For example, in *Icons from the World of Business*, Devangshu Dutta (2003) profiles ten highly successful first-generation entrepreneurs who have emerged from the Indian subcontinent. These include Sabeer Bhatia who "dreamt up Hotmail," Vinod Kapoor who "co-founded a great IT company Sun Microsystems and then funded a dozen ideas in another avatar as a venture capitalist," and B.M. Munjal who "led Hero group on a fifty-year journey from a small bicycle manufacturer to the top place in the global motorcycle industry." The author notes that, while they have success in widely different spheres, "Each is a risk-taker. All are workaholics, driven by ambitions that make the making of money almost incidental. Everyone has the useful capacity to develop and maintain stable long-term relationships with family and business contacts. All live well within their means. Most have religious or spiritual leanings" (2003: viii). In a companion publication entitled, *Business Gurus Speak*, S.N. Charry (2002) profiles another seven Indian business people including the following: Kiran Azumdar-Shaw, chairman and managing director of Biocon India Group; Azim Premji, chairman and managing director of Wipro; and N.R. Narayana Murthy, chairman and CEO of Infosys Technologies Ltd. Dutta observes:

> They have got themselves aligned with the international needs, inter-national standards of quality, cost and timeliness. While living in India, where excellence in products/services was quite irrelevant, these great minds of business benchmarked their firms against the practices globally. That is the beauty to behold in their endeavors . . . They have been a hopeless minority, but they stuck to their mission and values with almost

religious zeal and have demonstrated as to how business done with sense of mission, values and ethics can produce extraordinary results even in a vitalized economic atmosphere as in our country and how business should be done with lofty ideals. They are true patriots. What follows is in salutation to these extraordinary persons.

(Dutta 2003: 16–17)

What is interesting from reading both of these books is the emphasis that is placed on how well these leaders performed, even under the strictures of international comparison, despite an unpromising business environment. There is also a sense of patriotic duty that these individuals have performed on behalf of the nation. It is not just a question of creating profitable companies, there is also a requirement that they raise the bar throughout the country that other compatriot business leaders need to respond to. The made-in-American business celebrity phenomenon has been disseminated and has taken root with interesting local variations in countries throughout the world.

Brad Jackson has attempted to do a similar kind of thing in New Zealand with his book, *The Hero Manager*, which he co-authored with Ken Parry (Jackson and Parry 2001). Having both recently arrived in New Zealand, Jackson and Parry had been struck by their distinctive and favorable encounters as customers with several organizations and wanted to understand how the organizations had become that way. In the book they featured nine chief executives who had "demonstrated evidence of successfully bringing about dramatic and much-needed change to one or several large organizations over a sustained period while receiving considerable media attention" (2001: 33). The primary purpose for writing this book was encapsulated in the book's subtitle "Learning from New Zealand's Top Chief Executives." The argument ran as follows: almost all exemplars of business leadership in New Zealand traditionally came from overseas, most notably from the United States. Jackson and Parry questioned to what extent these exemplars were relevant to a country which had a remarkably different economic structure and was situated within a distinctive sociocultural context. In order to inspire future "made-in-New Zealand" leaders they felt the need to present exemplars and tell stories of individuals who had grown up in New Zealand and gone on to play a leading role in transforming organizations.

The choice of the "Hero Manager" title was chosen deliberately to provoke because most of the nation's celebrity leaders tend to originate from the realms of sports and the arts. Indeed, the authors detected an underlying sentiment of suspicion and distrust verging on open hostility to business leaders which apparently traced its lineage back to the financial crash of 1987 when many New Zealanders lost their life savings in shady get-rich-quick schemes, but is fundamentally a hallmark of the country's proudly egalitarian society. This hostility became considerably less veiled when Jackson and Parry participated in interviews with the media across the country. Much is made in New Zealand of the "Tall Poppy Syndrome," which describes the tendency for the media and their followers to keep those who have succeeded in whatever field firmly in their place (Mouly and Sankaran 2000). Anyone who appears to be getting "ideas above their station" is firmly chopped down, much in keeping with the "backlash" phenomenon that was discussed in the previous chapter.

What Jackson and Parry found most instructive from the whole exercise was how reluctant the hero managers were in being labeled "hero managers." Even when they explained the rationale for the title, they found it was a major disincentive to participating in the book. Thanks to the encouragement and endorsement of a singularly influential figure in New Zealand business, the chief executives agreed to participate. This was not just a case of false modesty, although New Zealanders do a very special line in self-deprecation. Their hesitancy stemmed from the assumption embedded in the notion of a hero manager that they alone were responsible for the successful leadership of their companies when they were at pains to stress the importance of the collective leadership of all of their employees.

Another surprise was how willing people were to tell the authors without being solicited, what the selected hero managers were "really like." In fact, Jackson and Parry frequently quipped, when giving talks about the book, that they had learned more about these chief executives after they published the book than beforehand and looked forward to publishing a second, greatly expanded edition! What they learned was the obvious—they had completely ignored the followers' perspectives on these leaders. They also experienced a fair amount of skepticism as well as criticism, most of it good natured, from their academic colleagues that they had reinforced a heroic model of leadership which was outmoded, hopelessly romantic, politically naïve and, from some quarters, morally reprehensible. It is to this critique that we now turn.

The post-heroic critique of heroic leadership

In the past decade, inspired partially by the "CEO backlash" that was discussed in Chapter 5 and driven in part by a lingering resentment and suspicion of hierarchical authority, a growing number of leadership and organizational scholars in tandem with a community of management consultants have launched a critique of the predominant heroic leadership models that have been promoted in hero manager accounts. The critique has essentially taken three separate, yet related thrusts. The first thrust emphasizes the need to develop a new model of leadership, generally dubbed "post-heroic" leadership (Fletcher 2004), that acknowledges and responds to the qualitatively different context within which contemporary organizations have to work. Post-heroic models of leadership recognize that effectiveness in knowledge-based environments depends less on the heroic actions of a few individuals at the top of the organization and more on collaborative leadership practices distributed throughout it (Manz and Sims 1991). What has emerged from these commentators is a less individualist, more relational concept of leadership; one that focuses on dynamic, interactive processes of influence and learning intended to transform organizational structures, norms, and work practices. Huey and Sookdeo (1999) typify the evangelical passion that suffuses those heralding a new post-heroic leadership dawn. They argue in a no-holds-barred polemic style that post-heroic leadership will challenge the very definition of corporate leadership for the twenty-first century, stating:

> The pressure is building to walk the talk. Call it whatever you like: post-heroic leadership, servant leadership, distributed leadership or to suggest a tag, virtual leadership. But don't dismiss it as just another touchy-feely flavor of the month. It's real, it's radical, and it's challenging the very definition of corporate leadership for the 21st century.
>
> (Huey and Sookdeo 1999: 42)

A second thrust of the critique of heroic leadership is less concerned with its instrumental limitations and more preoccupied with political and ideological concerns. In their survey of political leadership philosophy, Rejai and Phillips (2004) note that, with the exception of Rousseau and Marx, political philosophers have tended to present incomplete and deceptive ideas of leadership which have focused exclusively upon the leader and his ability to impose his vision upon his followers. Underpinning these ideas of leadership has been an underlying negative conception of human nature. For example, Plato's "Philosopher-King" is deliberately set apart from the people, his primary function being the administration of justice through the establishment of harmony between the parts of the soul (reason, spirit, and appetite) and the other classes of individuals (rulers, soldiers, and artisans). The creation of a shared vision does not exist.

This is a theme that is taken up in the contemporary context in a singularly virulent critique that has come from Gemmill and Oakley (1992). They argue that the conception of heroic leadership perpetuated and reinforced by business celebrities is a "myth" that functions to reinforce existing social beliefs and structures about the necessity of hierarchy and leaders in organizations. Taking a lead from the cultural studies' critique of celebrity that was discussed in Chapter 2, hero manager worship serves to repress, alienate, and "dumb down" individuals' desire to act independently and work for societal change. They note with more than a hint of bittersweet irony:

> The recent fascination with leadership characteristics and traits in the management literature is reminiscent of a ghost dance, an attempt to resurrect the spirit of time gone by. Ghost dances were a predominant expression of religious movements that gained popularity among Native American tribes in the later half of the nineteenth century in reaction to the impending destruction of their way of life.
>
> (Gemmill and Oakley 1992: 118)

Rather than providing the visionary future-oriented leadership that they purport to, hero managers may be simply helping managers to look back to a bygone era that is on the verge of extinction.

The third thrust of the critique of notions of heroic leadership is that they have never been appropriate, irrespective of context (post-industrial, industrial, or pre-industrial), because they have only ever provided a partial and one-sided account of leadership. Explanations of heroic leadership focus on the apex of the organization, privileging the significance of one individual—the CEO or chair—to the exclusion of all others. In his book *Leadership: Limits and Possibilities*, Grint (2005) suggests that leadership has traditionally been understood in four different ways: Leadership as Person (is it *who* "leaders" are that makes them leaders?); Leadership as Results (is it *what* "leaders" achieve that makes them leaders?); Leadership as Position (is it *where* "leaders" operate that makes them leaders?); and Leadership as Process (is it *how* "leaders" get things done that makes them leaders?). In Grint's view, each of these ways of thinking about leadership or "lenses" is valid and potentially useful. In fact, when we endeavour to make sense of leadership we should ensure that we view it through all four of these lenses.

The model of heroic leadership that is embedded in the accounts of business celebrities looks at leadership primarily through the "Positional" lens (i.e., it is concerned exclusively with those who run large and significant private-sector organizations), the underlying idea being that the titular leader is the one who is most directly responsible for determining organizational success or failure. Business celebrity accounts also apply the "Results" lens in that they tend to concentrate solely on those who have led organizations that have indeed achieved remarkable results during their tenure. In making sense of these results they also apply the "People" lens by identifying the key personal characteristics that make this individual so special, such as his or her courage, ambition, resilience, determination, intelligence, and communication skills.

Put very simply, the underlying logic that underpins the hero manager narrative broadly follows the same sequence: because of the hero manager's special characteristics they are appointed to the top position within the organization. Because of their special qualities the organization then becomes very successful. Grint makes the case that these all-pervasive and highly persuasive celebrified accounts of heroic leadership have led us to over-estimate the importance of the role of individual leaders, especially those who are given formal authority to run those organizations. This does not mean, however, that we have overestimated the significance of leadership within the organization, for this is something that should never be underestimated. Grint (2005) believes we have become overly pre-occupied with individual leaders when, in fact, we should have been focusing more on the long taken-for-granted and largely uncelebrated role of the "follower" (Chaleff 2002; Shamir *et al.* 2007; Kellerman 2008).

As a result of this multi-pronged critique, we can begin to appreciate the limitations of the heroic leadership model that is argued to permeate celebrity business leader accounts, but what kind of post-heroic leadership model might be developed in place of this? Pure versions of post-heroic models of leadership are technically neither leader-centered nor follower-centered because they reject the distinction between leaders and followers. Leadership is seen not as a role, but as a function or an activity that can be shared among members of a group or organization. Fundamentally, at the core of this approach is a belief that followers can and should be given their chance to lead, as it is not only the right thing to do but also the smartest thing to do. Traditional command-and-control, hierarchically based organizations that are purported to be celebrated in hero manager texts are seen as being no match for the flat, laterally integrated network organizations in the context of a rapidly changing competitive global economy.

We can best think of the various theories which advocate that followers should act as leaders along a continuum. At the more conservative end of the continuum is the notion of "co-leadership" which recognizes that leadership is rarely the preserve of one individual but is frequently exercised by a pair of individuals (Heenan and Bennis 1999) or shared by a group of individuals such as a top management team (Pearce and Conger 2003; Alvarez and Svejenova 2005). Further along the continuum is "shared leadership," the notion that the responsibility for guiding a group can rotate among its members, depending on the demands of the situation and the particular skills and resources required at that moment (Raelin 2003). Even further along the continuum is the notion of "distributed leadership" in which the team leads its work collectively by creating norms of behavior, contribution, and performance and by supporting each other and maintaining the morale of the group (Day *et al.* 2002).

Post-heroic models of leadership tend to be more normative than descriptive. They talk about how things should be rather than how they necessarily are. However, case studies of exemplary practice are enthusiastically presented from companies as diverse as law firms, car manufacturers, and IT service providers as evidence that shared and dispersed leadership are more than a gleam in the organizational theorist's eye. These forms of leadership do exist and can succeed but they are still distinguished by their rarity. While post-heroic leadership discourse has started to become mainstream among leadership scholars and many organizational development consultants, it is difficult to be neither categorical nor optimistic about the impact this discourse has on shaping the broader understanding of leadership and every-day workplace practices and norms. This kind of empirical investigation is still unfortunately rare.

However, a recent empirical study gives us pause for reflection. Drawing on research conducted with participants at various stages in two long-term leadership development programs, Carroll and Levy (2008) note that the managers they interviewed drew upon a blend of heroic and post-heroic discourses when discussing their experience and aspirations with respect to the way leadership was practiced in their organizations. Somewhat to their surprise, Carroll and Levy detected what they dubbed an "anti-heroic" discourse running through their discussions that was more constrained and cautious than the traditionally heroic discourse but more agentic than the post-heroic. They conclude:

> Post-heroism struggles to coherently confront the still dominant heroic viewpoint. From a discourse perspective, this can be attributed to its failure to offer a strong enough identity position and voice to actors to

claim and appropriate the leadership label. The discovery and development of an anti-heroic discourse, we argue, offers a more nuanced integration of the "best" of the heroic and post-heroic discourse.

(Carroll and Levy 2008: 3)

In the following section we will look at the efforts that have been made by a number of key proponents of this type of anti-heroic discourse. As we shall see, however, they might be more correctly characterized as promoting an "anti-celebrity" rather than an anti-heroic discourse.

The authentic and altrustic turn in heroic leadership

While the many leadership scholars described above have been advocating the replacement of the dominant and entrenched heroic model of leadership with more inclusive and collective "post-heroic" and distributed models of leadership, others have sought to redefine the qualities of genuinely heroic leaders. According to these scholars, the types of leaders whom we should ideally follow look nothing like the celebrities foisted upon us by the mass media. As opposed to advocates of distributed leadership, these scholars concede that organizational leaders will always exert a disproportionate amount of influence over their followers by virtue of their position of formal authority. For precisely this reason, the argument goes, it is vital to appoint the "right" kinds of leaders to such positions. And the right kinds of leaders are those who recognize that leadership is co-created by both leaders and followers. In this respect, these scholars attempt to integrate the best of the heroic and the post-heroic models as described by Carroll and Levy. In effect, they advocate not an anti-heroic model of leadership, but a heroic model that is anti-celebrity. As Morris *et al.* (2005) observe: "the notion of the celebrity CEO as heroic stands in sharp contrast to the traditional notion of a hero, a person who is willing to make the personal sacrifices necessary so that others may benefit." A central quality of the anti-celebrity leader is humility which they define as "a personal orientation founded on a willingness to see the self accurately and a propensity to put oneself in perspective" (2005: 1331). Authentically humble leaders understand their strengths, weaknesses, and limitations, and recognize how dependent they are on forces outside of themselves.

The popular quest for the authentically humble leader can be traced back to Robert Greenleaf's notion of the "servant leader" (Greenleaf 1977).

Servant leaders approach the leadership role from a non-focal position and seek to fulfill the interests of the organization and its members rather than maximize personal ambition. Rather than engaging in behaviors aimed at self-gratification or glorification as would the celebrity CEO, servant leaders work in a facilitative manner to ensure the betterment of the entire organization. The servant leader motif can be traced through a number of subsequent conceptions of leadership which all emphasize the humble leader's role in helping or empowering their followers to learn how to lead, such as Manz and Sims' (1991) notion of "Superleadership" and Badaracco's (2002) conception of "Quiet Leadership."

Arguably, Jim Collins has (2001a, 2001b) done the most to popularize and legitimize the importance of humility in leadership. He notes that "our misguided confusion of celebrities and leadership is neither right nor healthy. If we allow the celebrity model of leadership to triumph, we'll see the decline of our organizations" (2008: 20). In his richly anecdotal study of long-term organizational performance, Collins and his research team distinguish between a handful of consistently "great" companies and a much larger group of merely "good" organizations. Each of the nine "great" companies that were identified was led by a humble CEO who had invariably worked himself up to the top of the organization. Compared to the type of "level 4 leadership" that is exhibited by celebrated charismatic CEOs, Collins describes these CEOs as being "level 5 leaders" who, by contrast, are as follows:

> A study in duality: they are modest and willful, shy and fearless. They act with quiet, calm determination, and they rely principally on inspired standards, not inspiring charisma, to motivate. They channel their ambition into the company, not the self. They also "look in the mirror, not the window," to apportion responsibility for bad results, never blaming other people, external factors or bad luck. Similarly, they look out of the window to apportion credit for the company's success to employees, external factors or good luck.
>
> (Collins 2001b: 75)

It is somewhat ironic to observe that the relationship between humility and leadership has been considered primarily in the popular press rather than through academic research (Morris *et al.* 2005). The notable exception to this would be a rapidly expanding group of leadership scholars who are actively theorizing and empirically testing the notion of authentic leadership. Rooted in positive psychology (Seligman and Csikszentmihalyi 2000), a group of scholars based at the Gallup Institute of Leadership in Lincoln, Nebraska has advanced authentic leadership as a means to countervail the decreased confidence in and increased suspicion of leaders engendered by the celebrity CEO backlash described in the previous chapter. They conclude that they are "struck by the uplifting effects of lower profile but genuine leaders who lead by example in fostering healthy ethical climates characterized by transparency, trust, integrity, and high moral standards. We call such leaders authentic leaders who are not only true to themselves, but lead others by helping them to likewise achieve authenticity" (Gardner *et al.* 2005: 344).

Most of the initial work on authentic leadership has focused on clarifying the various constructs that underlie authentic leadership and developing a valid and reliable scale for measuring leaders' levels of authentic leadership from the perspective of followers. There is still a dearth of studies that have empirically explored this concept and its claims in any major or systematic way. Authentic leadership commands ready face validity and holds not inconsiderable rhetorical appeal. After all, who is going to stand up in favor of "inauthentic leadership"? Bill George, the former chairman and chief executive of Medtronic, a global medical technology firm, has done a great deal to promote the idea of authentic leadership to the practitioner audience though his book, naturally entitled *Authentic Leadership*, which traces his personal journey in turning around an ailing company and begins with the realization that "leadership is authenticity, not style" (George 2003).

The authentic turn in heroic leadership has been closely associated with an altruistic turn in business leadership. Eerily echoing the widely heralded philanthropic activities of the Robber Barons of the early part of the twentieth century discussed in the opening chapter of the book, we are witnessing a remarkably similar movement at the beginning of this century. In 2005, *Time* magazine selected Bill and Melinda Gates along with Bono as the "Person of the Year" in recognition of the creation of their $31 billion foundation (see Figure 4.3). In the following year, *The Economist* devoted a special survey to philanthropy, noting that "giving away money has never been so fashionable among the rich and famous," a development they dubbed "Philanthro-capitalism" (*The Economist* 2006). The combination of authentic and altruistic leadership is most famously encapsulated by Warren Buffet, who recently supplanted Bill Gates as the world's richest man, to become the most archetypal business celebrity of the first decade of the twenty-first century. His low-key and frugal ways are the stuff of legend. Buffet has lived in the same house, valued at about $685,000, since 1958 and has pledged to give away

Figure 6.1   Hillary Clinton enlists Warren Buffet in discussion on inheritance tax, December 12, 2007.

Source: Reproduced with the gracious permission of photographer Bill Wilson (http://billwilsonphotos.com)

85 percent of his total wealth over time, most of it to the Bill and Melinda Gates charitable foundation. The rest will go to four family charities. Reporting on the annual shareholder meeting of Berkshire Hathaway, known as the "Woodstock of Capitalism," *The Times* noted, "On the surface there is something surreal about 31,000 people flying across the world to see these elderly men talk about finance. But, more than anybody else, they represent a human face of business that people can relate and aspire to" (Bawden 2008: 39).

Graphically demonstrating the synergies that can be pervasively achieved between consultant gurus and hero managers, Charles Handy describes this philanthropic turn as "the new generosity." His book *The New Philanthropists* (Handy 2006) features interviews with and photographs of twenty-three individuals from "a new generation of practical philanthropists, men and women who have made their own fortunes and decided to move on from financial success to try to help those in need." They not only give money but also become very personally involved in the management of the organizations that they helped to create. Among the twenty-three are Tony Adams, a former soccer star, who has set up a clinic to help sports people with addictive problems, and Niall Mellon, an Irish properly developer who builds houses in the townships of South Africa along with Irish volunteers who are flown down expressly for this purpose. In explaining the rationale for this book, Handy observes:

> We believe that social change is often triggered when new role models begin to set a new fashion. For that to happen these new heroes have to be individuals with whom others can identify. Their personal stories should excite the imagination. They must be willing to put their heads above the parapet so that others can see them. We are both very grateful to those who put their heads above the parapet so that others can see them. They did so reluctantly, because they agreed with us that there should be more like them.
>
> (Handy 2006: 8)

In this statement Handy has neatly encapsulated the role and function of heroic leaders. He shows why heroic leaders will continue to persist in the face of the anti-heroic critique and the eloquently proposed variants of post-heroic notions of leadership. This is a theme to which we will return in the concluding chapter of this book. He also highlights a fundamental flaw in the efforts to rehabilitate the heroic model of leadership by foregrounding the authentic and altruistic qualities of leadership in order to outflank the celebrification processes.

Authentic heroic leadership emphasizes achievement, emulation, ethical judgment, and humility and rejects commodification, mediation, and attribution. However, viewed from the celebrity perspective, we can see that celebrification remains central to the successful promotion and adoption of this rehabilitated form of humble heroic leadership even though it is denied by those who produce this leadership product. This raises a central irony and recurrent theme of celebrity—namely, that the celebrated authentic leaders and their promoters and adherents deny their constructed nature. Here we have the apogee of celebrity leadership. Hero managers are leadership superstars who are in that position because of the ascription of their supposed superior individual qualities. But they are created in just the same way as academic and consultant management gurus and Hollywood stars, for that matter, are. Heroic leadership is celebrified leadership in denial of its own roots in the celebrity system.

Conclusion

In this chapter we have explored the connection between business celebrity and leadership; in particular we have been concerned with delineating the role played by business celebrities in the leadership industry and understanding their attendant influence upon the production and consumption of leadership. We have raised and begun to answer questions about the impact and significance of celebrification upon our understanding of, as well as our abilities to promote, the practice of leadership in an enlightened manner. For example, to what extent does celebrification impede or aid the practice of enlightened leadership? Is the celebrification of leadership an inevitable feature of a mass-mediated society? Is it possible to make celebrification a useful process in the promotion of better leadership theory and practice? To what extent is the quest for authentic or altruistic leadership a reaction to celebrification? Are these ideals of higher purpose leadership themselves doomed to become entangled in celebrification?

As we explored these questions, we discovered that in recent years the field of leadership studies has produced its own version of the business celebrity backlash. Many leadership scholars are becoming more and more adamant in their criticism of the usefulness of celebrity business leaders, and in their rejection of the kinds of heroic models of leadership implied by the very phenomenon of business celebrity itself. From the celebrity perspective developed in this book, however, these arguments appear misplaced for two important reasons. First of all, a blanket rejection of the idea of celebrity business leadership on the grounds that leadership is (or should be) a much more distributed and social process fails to appreciate the extent to which, as we argue throughout this book, the production and consumption of business celebrities are in fact fundamentally social phenomena involving the input and interaction of a variety of different concerned parties. Second, post-heroic critiques of celebrity business leadership do not fully recognize how the end products of the process of celebrification bear the marks of all of this social interaction. The fact that many celebrity business heroes themselves argue for more distributed and post-heroic styles of management points towards the manner in which business celebrities do not so much argue for heroic forms of leadership as much as they embody concerns and debates about what leadership should be like, and about how business institutions should be run.

We conclude that it would be better for leadership scholars and practitioners to engage in these debates than to simply dismiss them, ignore them, or hope that they will go away. Because they certainly show no signs of doing that. As we stated in the introductory chapter, while we do not intend to lionize business celebrities uncritically, or to hold them up as paragons of business virtue and acumen, we do intend for this book to help both academics and practitioners alike to learn from both negative critiques of business celebrity as well as positive appreciations of the manner in which celebrity business figures can motivate and inspire others.

7 The production of celebrities and the production of leadership

"He's the biggest celebrity in the world. But is he ready to lead?" The contrast between celebrity and leadership couldn't be painted much more starkly than in these two sentences, which opened one of several instantly infamous attack ads produced by the US presidential campaign of Republican Senator John McCain in the summer of 2008. The "he" in question, of course, was McCain's Democratic opponent, Senator Barack Obama. The ad, which the McCain campaign called "Celeb," sought to place a question mark over Obama's qualifications for the presidency by characterizing him as a mere celebrity. Toward this end it featured a rapid-fire montage of images and news footage: more than 100,000 Germans chanting Obama's name on the streets surrounding the Victory Column in Berlin; the disorienting flashes and pops of paparazzi cameras; Britney Spears making her way through some other crowd of onlookers; Paris Hilton posing frozen and aloof for a fashion shoot; and Obama himself striding confidently onto the podium to greet his German fans. The ad cut back and forth furiously between these images, but each individual piece of footage ran in slow motion in a way that created an impression of ominous foreboding (McCain Campaign, 2008).

The effect of the montage was to compare Barack Obama to Britney Spears and Paris Hilton. Like these two notoriously overexposed blondes, the ad insinuated, the flashy, young senator from Illinois should never be trusted to serve as president. By the very act of defining him as a celebrity, the ad declared him unfit for any such office. The implication behind the words and images was that because celebrities are merely false media constructions devoid of real accomplishment, ability, or authenticity, they are the polar opposite of "*real* leaders." Without even mentioning John McCain, the ad sought to remind voters that he, by contrast, was a real leader and a real hero, a Navy fighter pilot and decorated veteran of the Vietnam war who had been shot down over Hanoi, severely wounded, tortured, and held in a POW camp for nearly six years.

Although the "Celeb" spot was about a political rather than a business figure, it exemplifies several of the characteristics and dynamics we have located at the heart of the phenomenon of business celebrity throughout this book. It drew its rhetorical force from the instantly recognizable discourse of the anti-celebrity backlash as we have described it. It made its case primarily by means of visual images rather than words. It tied those images together by invoking a common complaint about the lack of substance behind the celebrity facade. That kind of complaint rests ultimately on the same logic that leadership scholars and others use to dismiss celebrity business leaders and to champion "real heroes" and various forms of post-heroic leadership.

The fact that the "Celeb" ad formed part of a presidential campaign further underscores our main point in this book. Although such campaigns revolve around the attempt to elect a singular individual to high office, they are not possible without the efforts and contributions of a vast array of actors and intermediaries. And political candidates bear the mark of all these various inputs and interactions. They do not so much stand for distinct positions as they embody debates and arguments over such positions, because in today's high-voltage political environment, one voter's champion is another voter's anathema. Presidential campaigns are debates over not only who should run a society, but how it should be run. By the same token, as we have pointed out, business celebrities are best understood not as self-made corporate superheroes, but rather as the complex and multivalent end products of an often contentious process of celebrification. Like political candidates also, business celebrities function as forums for dialogue, flashpoints for debate, and battlefields for conflict over what our society should be like—with respect to business rather than politics—and what kinds of people should lead it.

In this book we have sought to demystify the manner in which business celebrities come to serve this symbolic, cultural function. We have described in detail the crowded and dynamic industrial processes that invest certain notable business figures with their exalted status. We have pointed out that business celebrities are not simply well-known persons, but elaborate constructions that would not exist as celebrities save for the intervention and interaction of a variety of different actors and intermediaries. On this basis we have defined business celebrity as the orchestrated co-production, cross-promotion, and circulation of exemplary business personalities via a wide range of media platforms and channels. The celebrity business leaders generated by this process—the Richard Bransons, the Jack Welches, the Martha

Stewarts, and the Donald Trumps—achieve widespread and self-perpetuating media exposure to the point where narratives and images of their actions, personalities and/or private lives play a major role in debates and struggles over what it means to be a leader and to take action in a society dominated by business forces and institutions beyond individual control.

As we explained in Chapter 2, our theoretical approach to the phenomenon of business celebrity combines the "production of culture" perspective as developed in sociology and cultural studies with "the romance of leadership" perspective as developed in research on management and organization. We noted that scholars working from the former perspective have provided a compelling analysis of the celebrity business but have neglected to consider how the particular case of *business* celebrities might strengthen their analysis. Scholars working from the latter perspective have looked closely at business celebrities but, ironically, have downplayed the significance of the business dynamics that produce them. By combining these two perspectives, we have explained how the construction and promotion of celebrity leaders are carried out not by any one sector or set of actors, but by a variety of loosely coupled third parties and intermediaries who work at cross-purposes as often as they collaborate. In this manner we have developed an explanatory framework that makes clear how the process of celebrification works, and what effect it has on the nature of the celebrities it produces.

The strength of our approach is that it stresses the crowded and interactive nature of the celebrification process, and the multivalent nature of the celebrities that result from it. There is not one celebrity industry, but a number of loosely coupled industries that contribute to the process of celebrification. The production of any given celebrity requires not just one well-oiled publicity machine, but a whole network of interlocking publicity and media engines running in tandem. It requires the efforts of many different kinds of cultural intermediaries, including journalists, editors, photographers, publicists, agents, public relations professionals, talk-show hosts, video producers, filmmakers, and even other celebrities. And it is crucial to remember that the process of celebrification is not complete without the active participation of fans, audience members, and media consumers. According to our framework, the interactions between these various parties are characterized by the dynamics of *attribution*, *access*, *mediation*, and *traction*.

As previous research on celebrity in organization and management studies has made clear, business celebrities are highly valued in large part because journalists *attribute* them with special qualities, skills, capabilities, and insights. But, as we point out, it is also important to recognize that the value of celebrities depends just as much on the manner in which various cultural intermediaries and go-betweens restrict and control *access* to them. These issues of access also highlight the importance of the dynamics of *mediation* to the construction of celebrity—by which term we refer to the crucial shaping role played by the many individuals, organizations, and institutions that act as promotional agents, boundary spanners, and gatekeepers. Finally, the efforts of these many parties are not sufficient to cause the necessary elements to crystallize into the phenomenon we call celebrity without that relatively unpredictable and elusive dynamic we called *traction*. With this term we refer to the fact that the burgeoning celebrity needs to find a foothold at different points all along the celebrification process by appealing simultaneously to many different and often conflicting interests and agendas. As we have discussed, traction is especially important among fans, audiences, and media consumers. The centrality of traction to the celebrity phenomenon helps explain why celebrities are multivalent, and seem to contain multiple personalities. They must do so in order to appeal to so many different publics and interests.

With these issues in mind, we then proceeded to provide a number of detailed examples of how our explanatory framework helps to make sense of business celebrities. In Chapter 3 we highlighted the importance of speaking events and performances to the celebrity status of management gurus such as Tom Peters, Gary Hamel, and Stephen Covey. We also interviewed publishing industry players and other experts to understand the manner in which blockbuster management advice books are produced. The creation of management advice best-sellers is a process of celebrification carried out by a variety of business culture intermediaries. While the authors/gurus are central to this process in a symbolic sense, they need not function as the driving force behind the books published in their name. While the nature of their live performances would lead us to characterize these gurus as something more akin to shamans, we concluded that the elaborate network of business culture intermediaries necessary to produce business best-sellers makes clear that such guru figures are best understood as management fashion celebrities.

In Chapter 4 we examined portraits, photographs, and other visual images of celebrity CEOs. The centrality of visual representation to the celebrity system requires the cultivation of a form of "visual literacy" in order to "read" the omnipresent iconography of business celebrity. A closer look at business celebrities from such a perspective helped bring into focus the construction of multiple, often conflicting images of the same business celebrity figure;

the manner in which even individual images invite multiple perspectives and conflicting interpretations; and the involvement of multiple actors and interests in relational processes of image production, dissemination, and interpretation. Conflicts over how we should interpret such images of business celebrity came to the fore in Chapter 5. We revealed the tenuous nature of individual claims to business celebrity by examining the recurrent phenomenon that we have called the CEO celebrity backlash. We also argued that antipathy towards celebrity figures actually functions as a crucial component of the process of celebrification, and ultimately contributes to the phenomenon of business celebrity over the long term.

In Chapter 6 we explored the connections between business celebrity and leadership. We found that many leadership scholars are becoming more and more adamant in their criticism of celebrity business leaders, and in their rejection of the kinds of heroic models of leadership implied by the very phenomenon of business celebrity itself. From the celebrity perspective developed in this book, however, we argue that these arguments are misplaced, because both critics and advocates of the notion of heroic leadership turn their back on the celebrification process. Critics attack the celebrity rather than the complex and distributed web of producers and consumers that creates and sustains the hero. Advocates insist that true business heroes do not need the media, do not crave media attention, and do not really worry about what people think about them. With its emphasis on achievement, authenticity, and humility, the notion of heroic leadership represents an implicit critique of the very notion of celebrity we have described in this book.

The notion that heroism is authentic, while celebrity is fake, animates a lot of discussions about the celebrity phenomenon. It also animates the McCain campaign "Celeb" ad that we discussed above. In fact, that ad rests ultimately on the same logic that leadership scholars and others use to dismiss celebrity business leaders and to champion "real heroes" and various forms of post-heroic leadership. Gamson has called this logic "the story of celebrity manufacture" (1994: 143). It is a powerful logic, as exemplified by the fact that it informs the most famous thing ever said about the phenomenon of celebrity: Boorstin's argument that celebrities are primarily famous for being famous. According to Gamson, the logic calls into question the notion that celebrities *actually do* anything to deserve all the media attention and adulation they receive. From this perspective celebrity is a function of *technique* rather than *merit*, of media manipulation rather than accomplishment. "The story of celebrity manipulation and manufacture, by potentially undermining the ability to decode the text as anything *but* artifice, can potentially be mobilized to subvert rather than support the story of deserved, internally driven fame," says Gamson (1994: 144). By prying open the curtain to reveal the mechanisms of celebrification, the McCain campaign sought to use this story of celebrity manufacture to question whether Barack Obama had ever really done anything (other than manipulating the media) that would qualify him as a serious candidate for the presidency.

But the McCain campaign perhaps failed to take into account that this kind of celebrity exposé has become somewhat of a cliché. The story of celebrity manufacture fails to evoke a sense of outrage or scandal anymore because contemporary media culture is constantly in the process of exposing—and even celebrating—the workings of celebrification, primarily for entertainment purposes. How else can we explain the enormous appeal of reality shows like *American Idol*, *Big Brother*, *X Factor*, or *Dancing with the Stars*? They do not attempt to conceal or mystify the fact that celebrities are manufactured by a crowded media process. To the contrary, such shows attract attention by laying bare the media conventions that can make any ordinary person look like a celebrity—or vice versa. High viewer ratings and levels of audience participation in voting contests related to such shows would suggest that people enjoy participating in the process of celebrification (Carter 2008).

As if to underscore this point, in September, 2008 the comedy website *Funny or Die* produced a series of satiric video responses to the McCain "Celeb" ad, poking fun at the conventions that can make even a leggy socialite like Paris Hilton look presidential (Szymanski *et al.* 2008). In the spoofs Hilton herself took offense at "that wrinkly, white-haired dude" (McCain) and declared her own candidacy for "fake president." The first spot opened with the same Berlin crowd footage as the original "Celeb" ad, but with a voice-over that declared, "He's the oldest celebrity in the world—like, *super* old —but is he ready to lead?" Stretched out in a bikini and high heels on a reclining lawn chair, Hilton presented her own (surprisingly coherent) energy policy, and concluded, "I want America to know that I'm, like, *totally* ready to lead." The "Paris Does Politics" ads were funny. They probably did not convince many people that the blonde heiress and erstwhile amateur pornography video star would make a good president. But they did highlight the fact that our culture has become too savvy about the way celebrities get constructed to be taken in for too long by the anti-celebrity arguments advanced by the McCain campaign. They also highlighted the fact that there are many possible ways to respond to the manner in which the mechanics of celebrification have become such a visible and dominant part of the media environment. (See Figure 7.1.)

On the basis of extensive conversations with celebrity watchers themselves, Gamson divides these possible responses into four general categories. There will always be people, he points out, who either cannot or refuse to notice the mechanics of celebrity production. These are the true believers in this or that celebrity, the traditionalists for whom "Fame is a process in which natural merits are recognized and rewarded" (Gamson 1994: 159). This kind of celebrity watcher might argue, for example, that Bill Gates is the most visible and photographed business person on the planet because he deserves to be so. "Second order traditionalists," Gamson maintains, acknowledge the artificiality of the process that produces celebrities, but admire them nonetheless. For these people, Gamson says, "merit is preserved despite a revelation of artificial techniques" (1994: 147), often times by distinguishing between phony or "wannabe" celebrities and those who really deserve their fame. From this perspective one might argue that Donald Trump is a self-promoting fake who cannot stop himself from mugging for the cameras, but that Steve Jobs is a true genius whose media poses and theatrical product launches are completely justified.

Figure 7.1 "Paris Does Politics." A still image from a comedy video created by the website *Funny or Die* at http://www.funnyordie.com. Reproduced with permission from the Associated Press.

Gamson's third category of celebrity watcher consists of those people who think that all celebrities are phonies, and that the exposure of the celebrification techniques and processes proves their point. Gamson includes in this group those "postmodernists" who believe that media manipulation has taken over contemporary society to the point where there is no real person of substance behind any celebrity façade. Finally, Gamson says, there are many celebrity watchers who maintain an ironic distance from the phenomenon, but still appreciate it for what it is. He calls this group the game players, people who actively consume and manipulate celebrity media texts according to their fancy. "Their involvement may be based on pleasures that simply bypass the questions of claims to fame or that even make use of both the stories and the ambiguity they together create," he explains. "These audiences use celebrities not as models or fantasies but as opportunities: to play freely with the issues they embody (the construction of the self in public, for example)" (1994: 148).

When it comes to business celebrity, most scholars of leadership and management have taken one of the first three positions Gamson describes. Many have chosen to ignore the process of celebrification and maintain a true believer stance towards the achievements and merits of great business leaders. Some have carved out a position as second-order traditionalists, acknowledging the power of the celebrity industries but insisting that certain great leaders can still rise above the fray. Those others may amount to mere celebrities, so this argument goes, but Jack Welch or Bill Gates or Richard Branson are true business heroes. The problem with these two traditionalist perspectives is that they require one to ignore many of the dynamics of celebrity building we have discussed in this book. In order to hold business leaders up on a pedestal like the true believers do, that eye has to systematically de-celebrify them—that is, to ignore the actions and interactions of the many other people that work so hard to keep the hero elevated above everyone else. Some scholars and observers who approach these matters in the tradition of critical management studies might choose to do the opposite. That is, they seize upon the false nature of the façade of celebrification to adopt a postmodernist or anti-believer stance, and to deny the existence of any substance behind the celebrity spectacle whatsoever.

Our own approach in this book has been to adopt the insights available from this latter, critical perspective, but without the kind of skepticism that would lead one to dismiss traditionalist or second-order true believers as a matter of course. And our emphasis on the manner in which business celebrities function as multivalent or malleable figures that are mobilized in different ways in the context of different debates reflects Gamson's description of the game-playing perspective. From this perspective, as we discussed in our chapter on the many competing images of celebrity CEOs, there are almost as many Jack Welches as there are people who have an opinion of the former GE superstar. From this perspective also, heroic leadership is in the eye of the beholder. The strength of the game-playing perspective is that it acknowledges the crowded process of celebrification, and brings into sharp focus the many business cultural intermediaries that make heroic leadership possible.

Let's face it, no matter how much we insist upon their many fine achievements, or their authenticity, or their humility, heroic leaders and guru heroes are still elaborate media productions. Otherwise, we would never even hear about them. Except on the personal level of everyday interaction, it is not possible to have a business hero who is not also a media phenomenon. They are not *like* business celebrities, they *are* business celebrities. But this fact does not invalidate them or take away from their value. We can learn a lot from hero managers and academic and consultant gurus precisely because of, rather than in spite of, the fact that they depend on the efforts of so many others to achieve and maintain their lofty position. As business celebrities, hero managers embody and perpetuate debates and conflicts over what leadership should be, over how our business institutions and our society should be run. If we ignore the many voices and interests that contribute to these debates—if we ignore, that is, the process of celebrification itself—then we cannot understand the significance of business heroes and celebrities in contemporary society.

We will end this book with a discussion about the implications of our study of celebrity for future research on leadership. Like the McCain ad we discussed at the beginning of this concluding chapter, much of leadership research has tried to paint a stark contrast between the flash of celebrity and the true nature of authentic leadership. On the basis of our investigation in this book, we would argue the opposite case. That is, celebrity is actually a lot like leadership, and the explanatory framework we have developed in this book can provide a model for a new approach to the study of leadership itself. Drawing on our discussion of the production of business celebrity, we intend to develop a new approach to studying the production of leadership and the leadership industries. From this perspective, we intend to conduct empirical research and build new theory around the proposition that it is important to understand leadership as a product of the many organizational, promotional, and discursive practices that characterize the leadership industries. We intend to explore the close, mutually determining relationship between practical and theoretical approaches to leadership on the one hand, and the creation and promotion of leadership products and services via the leadership industries on the other.

We are not the first scholars to observe that leadership is the product of a set of industrial practices and dynamics. But those scholars who have introduced this idea before have done so mainly to criticize the very idea of leadership itself (Barker 2001; Sinclair 2007). While we share many of the critical concerns voiced by these scholars, we do not agree that the mere fact that leadership is a cultural commodity counts as a criticism in and of itself, and certainly not as a reason to dismiss the idea of leadership altogether. From a production of leadership perspective, leadership is not merely an empirical object to be studied, a set of desirable characteristics to be developed, or a collection of best practices to be disseminated by leadership scholars, trainers, coaches, or consultants. In fact, the diverse activities of these and many other actors and institutions all contribute in a direct and substantive manner to the production of leadership itself, both as an intellectual concept and as a cultural commodity. This means that it is not strictly accurate to talk about "leadership" in the singular, because it consists of a variety of different products, services, and theoretical formulations.

One important step towards theorizing the production of leadership will be to do some basic industry analysis. What are the origins of the leadership industries, and how have they developed historically? How significant are they in terms of volume, profits, and personnel? What kinds of opportunities, constraints, and institutional dynamics shape the market for leadership products and services? How are these industries structured and segmented? Who are the key players, and how do they position themselves? What kinds of results are they supposed to produce, and how effective are they at actually doing so? To begin answering such questions, we can build on what we know from the study of similar industrial systems, and from the celebrity industries in particular. Leadership is not a mass-produced, durable item, like an automobile or a toaster, and the leadership industries do not operate according to a centralized logic or a factory mode of production. The design, manufacture, and promotion of leadership products are organized in a manner that resembles more closely the production of other cultural and symbolic goods and services by the cultural industries more generally.

Jones and Thornton (2005) have pointed out that the dynamics of the cultural industries are characteristic of professional service firms. As close cousins to such firms, the leadership industries also depend on the cultivation of "symbolic, creative and knowledge-based assets," and "create products that serve important symbolic functions such as capturing, refracting, and legitimating societal knowledge and values." From this perspective, the dynamics of the production of celebrity that we have discussed in this book are not a reason to dismiss celebrities as leaders, but rather a reason to further explore celebrity in order to mine the lessons it can provide about the production of leadership. The fact that the production of leadership is organized as a form of cultural production has many consequences, but at first glance several stand out as particularly important:

- *As with the production of celebrities, the production of leadership takes place via a number of distinct yet interrelated sub-industries and institutions.* Each of these has its own niche, its own strategic logic, and its own set of organizational dynamics. They are connected in a loosely coupled network characterized by cooperation, cross-fertilization, and competition. A partial list of these industries and institutions would include consulting; coaching; leadership training and development; commercial and academic publishing; business media and journalism; leadership education and research in universities and business schools at the undergraduate, masters, and executive levels; the guru-oriented leadership seminar and promotional event industry; and the burgeoning leadership institute industry.

- *Likewise, the production of leadership in these different contexts, as well as the interaction that occurs across these contexts, involves the active participation of a host of content providers, promotional entrepreneurs, boundary-spanners and gatekeepers.* These business culture intermediaries include authors, journalists, editors of newspapers, magazines, and academic journals, public relations representatives, agents, photographers, film-makers, academics, human relations professionals, coaches, trainers, seminar and conference organizers, consultants, and many others.

- *The consumption of leadership contributes to the production of leadership.* In this book we have stressed that fans, audiences, and media consumers are a crucial component of the process of celebrification. By the same token, leaders do not exist without followers, and the production of leadership cannot function without its own consuming audience made up of organizations, corporations, executives, MBAs, leadership enthusiasts on the street, and aspiring leaders of all sorts. And, especially since the products of the leadership industries are discourses of agency and power, it makes little sense to cast the consumers of those products as the passive recipients of a set of prepackaged goods.

- *The participation of so many different industries, actors, and end-users means that leadership actually consists of a range of different cultural and symbolic products and services which are difficult to categorize under any unitary definition or theoretical paradigm.* Again, this means that it is important for scholars and practitioners to recognize the existence of different "leaderships"—if only the word were not so awkward—different forms, theories, and practices of leadership that are context-specific and can either complement or contradict each other.

Far from representing the antithesis of authentic leadership, therefore, celebrity provides a crucial model for understanding how leadership itself is increasingly becoming a commercial product. The fact that leadership is a cultural commodity does not delegitimize its importance and usefulness for individuals, for organizations, or for society at large. Scholars of management fashions have spent a lot of time learning this same lesson. The notion that something is a management fashion or fad often serves as the grounds for dismissing its significance (Guthey *et al.* 2006). But imagine if organizations refused to adopt quality principles, or knowledge management practices, or corporate social responsibility initiatives, simply because such ideas and techniques had become caught up in the promotional machinery of the management fashion industries. As with management fashions, of course, there is good reason to be cautious about adopting programs heedlessly, or ignoring the dynamics of their promotion and hype. But, like the management fashion system, the system of celebrity production can equally serve as a resource for learning about new ideas and personalities, and as a sounding board for differing opinions, approaches, and debates about how organizations should be led into the future.

Like the study of management fashions, and like the study of business celebrities, the study of the production of leadership and the leadership industries can perform another invaluable service. It can serve to highlight the important role that leadership and organization scholars themselves play in the supply chain of leadership products and services. As teachers in undergraduate, masters, and executive programs in business schools, of course, they participate in the business of producing new leaders. And as researchers, they construct new discourses of leadership even as they study it, often generating content that filters further down the supply chain for distribution by various practitioners in the field. By taking account of the conditions of the ongoing production and reproduction of leadership, therefore, a fresh approach that draws on the lessons about celebrity we have uncovered in this book will contribute to the field of leadership studies a more reflexive sense of its own role in that process.

References

Abrahamson, E. (1996) "Management Fashion," *Academy of Management Review*, vol. 21, no. 1: 254–85.

Abrahamson, E. and Fairchild, G. (1999) "Management Fashion: Lifecycles, Triggers, and Collective Processes," *Administrative Science Quarterly*, vol. 44: 708–40.

Alvarez, J.L. and Svejenova, S. (2005) *Sharing Executive Power: Roles and Relationships at the Top*, Cambridge: Cambridge University Press.

Anderson, C.J. and Imperia, G. (1992) "The Corporate Annual Report: A Photo Analysis of Male and Female Portrayals," *Journal of Business Communication*, vol. 29, no. 2: 113–28.

Arnold, M., Benoit, B., and Munter, P. (2006) "Cartoons Draw Islamic Rage," *Financial Times*, 3 February: 1.

Badaracco, J.L. (2002) *Leading Quietly: An Unorthodox Guide to Doing the Right Thing*, Boston, MA: Harvard Business School Press.

Barker, R.A. (2001) "The Nature of Leadership," *Human Relations*, vol. 54, no. 4: 469–94.

Barlow, P. (1997) "Facing the Past and Present: The National Portrait Gallery and the Search for Authentic Portraiture," in Woodall, J. (ed.) *Portraiture: Facing the Subject*, Manchester: Manchester University Press: 219–38.

Barnard, C. (1938) *The Functions of the Executive*, Cambridge, MA: Harvard University Press.

Bastone, W. (ed.) (2008) "The Smoking Gun," http://www.thesmokinggun.com, last accessed on 23 April, 2009.

Baur, C. (1994) "Management Evangelists in Showbiz Arena," *Sunday Times*, 19 June.

Bawden, T. (2008) "Shareholders Laugh All the Way as Comedy Duo Play the Crowd," *Times*, 5 May: 39.

Baxandall, M. 1988. *Painting and Experience in Fifteenth Century Italy*, Oxford: Oxford University Press.

Becker, H.S. (1974) "Art as Collective Action," *American Sociological Review*, vol. 30, no. 6: 767–76.

Becker, H.S. (1982) *Art Worlds*, Los Angeles, CA: University of California Press.

Beloff, H. (1985) *Camera Culture*, Oxford: Basil Blackwell.

Benders, J. and van Veen, K. (2001) "What's a Fashion? Interpretative Viability and Management Fashions," *Organization*, vol. 8: 33–53.

Beniger, J. (1987) "Toward an Old New Paradigm: The Half-Century Flirtation with Mass Society," *Public Opinion Quarterly*, vol. 51, no. 2: S46–S66.

Benjamin, W. (2003) "Extracts from 'The Work of Art in the Age of Mechanical Reproduction,'" in Wells, L. (ed.) *The Photography Reader*, London: Routledge: 42–52.

Berg, P.O. (1985) "Organization Change as a Symbolic Transformation Process," in Frost, P., Moore, M.R., Lundberg, L.C. and Martin, J. (eds) *Reframing Organizational Culture*, Beverly Hills, CA: Sage: 281–300.

Berger, J. (1972) *Ways of Seeing*, London: BBC/Harmondsworth and Penguin.

Berle, A.A. and Means, G.C. (1967) *The Modern Corporation and Private Property*, revised edition, New York: Harcourt, Brace & World.

Berman, M. (1970) *The Politics of Authenticity: Radical Individualism and the Emergence of Modern Society*, New York: Atheneum.

Bernstein, D. (1984) *Company Image and Reality: A Critique of Corporate Communications*, Eastbourne, UK: Holt, Rinehart & Winston.

Bianco, A., Lavell, L., Merritt, J., and Barrett, A. (2000) "The CEO Trap," *BusinessWeek*, 11 December: 86ff.

Bianco, A., Symonds, W., and Byrnes, N. (2002) "The Rise and Fall of Dennis Kozlowski," *BusinessWeek*, 23 December: 64–6.

Bilton, N. (2005) "Untitled Photo Illustration," *New York Times*, 10 February: C1.

Bloomsbury Reference Book (2004) *Movers and Shakers: The People Behind Business Today*, London: Bloomsbury.

Blumer, H.G. (1968) "Fashion", in Sills, D.L. (ed.) *International Encyclopedia of the Social Sciences*, New York: Macmillan, vol. 5: 341–5.

Boorstin, D. (1961) *The Image: A Guide to Pseudo-Events in America*, New York: Vintage Books.

Bourdieu, P. (1984) *Distinction: A Social Critique of the Judgement of Taste*, translated by R. Nice, London: Routledge.

Brabeck-Letmathe, P. (1999) "Beyond Corporate Image: The Search for Trust," an address to the Oxford University European Affairs Society on 30 November.

Branson, R. (1999) *Losing My Virginity*, Sydney: Random House.

Branson, R. (2006) *Screw It, Let's Do It: Lessons in Life*, second edition, Sydney: Random House.

Braudy, L. (1997) *The Frenzy of Renown: Fame and Its History*, New York: Oxford University Press.

Burgoyne, J. (2004) "How Certain Are We that Management and Leadership Development Is Effective?," paper presented at the Management Learning and Leadership Workshop, Lancaster University, July.

Burns, J.M. (1978) *Leadership*, New York: Harper & Row.

Burrows, P. (2003) *Backfire: Carly Fiorina's High-Stakes Battle for the Soul of Hewlett-Packard*, New York: John Wiley.

BusinessWeek (1995) "Did Dirty Tricks Create a Best-seller?", 7 August: 30–3.

BusinessWeek (2001) "The Most Aggressive CEO," 28 May: 56ff.

BusinessWeek (2002) "The Top 25 Managers of the Year," 14 January: 52ff.

Byrne, J. (1998) "Jack: A Close-Up Look at How America's #1 Manager Runs GE," *BusinessWeek*, 8 June: 90.

Calder, B.J. (1977) "An Attribution Theory of Leadership," in Staw, B.M. and Salancik, G.R. (eds) *New Directions in Organizational Behavior*, Chicago, IL: St. Clair: 179–204.

Carlyle, T. (1910) *On Heroes and Hero Worship*, London: Ward, Lock.

Carroll, B. and Levy, L. (2008) "Discourses of the Heroic: Theorising the Anti-Hero," paper presented at the International Workshop on Leadership and Discourse, University of Sydney.

Carson, P.P., Lanier, P., Carson, K.D., and Guidry, B.N. (2000) "Clearing a Path Through the Management Fashion Jungle: Some Preliminary Trailblazing," *Academy of Management Journal*, vol. 43: 1143–58.

Carter, B. (2008) "Reality TV Is No Lightweight in the Battle to Outlast Strikers," *New York Times*, 14 January: 4.

Caulkin, S. (1997) "Quirky Common Sense at $95,000 a Day," *Observer* (Business Section), 13 April: 14.

Cenicola, T. and Best Jr., J.C. (2005) "Untitled Photo Illustration," *New York Times*, 13 February: C1.

Chaleff, I. (2002) *The Courageous Follower: Standing Up to and for Our Leaders*, San Francisco, CA: Berrett-Koehler.

Charry, S.N. (2002) *Business Gurus Speak*, Delhi: Macmillan.

Chen, C.C. and Meindl, J.R. (1991) "The Construction of Leadership Images in the Popular Press: The Case of Donald Burr and People Express," *Administrative Science Quarterly*, vol. 36, no. 4: 521–51.

Clark, T. and Greatbatch, D. (2002) "Collaborative Relationships in the Creation and Fashioning of Management Ideas: Gurus, Editors and Managers," in Kipping, M. and Engwall, L. (eds) *Management Consulting: Emergence and Dynamics of a Knowledge Industry*, Oxford: Oxford University Press: 129–45.

Clark, T. and Greatbatch, D. (2003) "Management Fashion as Image-Spectacle: The Production of Management Best-Sellers," *Management Communication Quarterly*, vol. 1, no. 4: 396–424.

Clark, T. and Salaman, G. (1996) "The Management Guru as Organizational Witchdoctor," *Organization*, vol. 3, no. 1: 85–107.

Clark, T. and Salaman, G. (1998) "Telling Tales: Management Gurus' Narratives and the Construction of Managerial Identity," *Journal of Management Studies*, vol. 35, no. 2: 137–61.

Collins, J. (2001a) *Good to Great: Why Some Companies Make the Big Leap and Others Don't*, London: Random House.

Collins, J. (2001b) "Level 5 Leadership," *Harvard Business Review*, vol. 79, no. 1: 66–76.

Collins, J. (2003) "The 10 Greatest CEOs of All Time," *Fortune*, 21 July: 54–68.

Collins, J. (2008) "Celebrity Leadership," *Leadership Excellence*, vol. 25, no. 1: 20.

Collins, J. and Porras, J.I. (1994) *Built to Last: Successful Habits of Visionary Companies*, New York: Harper Business.

Colvin, G. (1999) "The Ultimate Manager," *Fortune*, 22 November: 185–7.

Connor, S. (2005) "Defiling Celebrity," paper presented at the Cultural Histories of Celebrity seminar at the Humanities Research Centre at the University of Warwick, 24 October.

Czarniawska, B. (1997) *Narrating the Organisation: Dramas of Institutional Identity*, Chicago, IL: University of Chicago Press.

Davis, G. and McAdam, D. (2000) "Corporations, Classes, and Social Movements after Managerialism," in Staw, B. and Sutton, R.I. (eds) *Research in Organizational Behaviour*, Oxford: Oxford University Press, vol. 22: 195–238.

Day, D., Gronn, P., and Salas, E. (2004) "Leadership Capacity in Teams," *Leadership Quarterly*, vol. 15, no. 6: 857–80.

DePree, M. and Mahoney, R. (1996) "Backlash," *Across the Board*, vol. 33, no. 7: 24ff.

Diba, A. and Munoz, L. (2001) "America's Most Admired Companies," *Fortune*, vol. 143, no. 4 (19 February): 64.

Dougherty, D. and Kunda, G. (1990) "Photograph Analysis: A Method to Capture Organisational Belief Systems," in Pasquale, P. (ed.) *Symbols and Artifacts: Views of the Corporate Landscape*, Berlin: Walter de Gruyter: 185–206.

Du Gay, P. (1996) *Consumption and Identity at Work*, London: Sage.

Dutta, D. (2003) *Icons from the World of Business*, New Delhi: Puffin Books.

Dutton, J. and Dukerich, J. (1991) "Keeping an Eye on the Mirror: Image and Identity in Organisational Adaptation," *Academy of Management Review*, vol. 34: 517–54.

Dutton, J., Dukerich, J., and Harquail, C. (1994) "Organizational Images and Member Identification," *Administrative Science Quarterly*, vol. 39, no. 2: 239–63.

Eccles, R. and Nohria, N. (1994) *Beyond the Hype: Rediscovering the Essence of Management*, Cambridge, MA: Harvard Business School Press.

Eliade, M. (1964) *Shamanism: Archaic Techniques of Ecstasy*, translated by W. Trask, London: Routledge & Kegan Paul.

Evans, J. and Hesmondhalgh, D. (2005) *Understanding Media: Inside Celebrity*, London: Open University Press.

Ewen, S. (1996) *PR! A Social History of Spin*, New York: Basic Books.

Farnham, A. (2000) *Forbes Great Success Stories*, New York: John Wiley.

Fayol, H. (1949) *General and Industrial Management*, translated by C. Storrs, London: Pitman.

Fernandez, J.A. and Underwood, L. (2006) *China CEO*, Singapore: John Wiley.

Fingeroth, D. (2004) *Supermen on the Couch: What Superheroes Really Tell Us about Ourselves and Our Society*, New York: Continuum.

Fiske, J. (1989) *Understanding Popular Culture*, London: Routledge.

Fletcher, J.K. (2004) "The Paradox of Postheroic Leadership: An Essay on Gender, Power, and Transformational Change," *Leadership Quarterly*, vol. 15: 647–61.

Fombrun, C. and Van Riel, C. (1997) "The Reputational Landscape," *Corporate Reputation Review*, vol. 1, no. 1 and 2: 5–13.

Forbes (2007) "Forbes 400: The Richest People in America," 8 October.

Fortune (2002) "The Greedy Bunch: You Bought, They Sold," 2 September.

Frank, T. (1995) *The Conquest of Cool: Business Culture, Counterculture, and the Rise of Hip Consumerism*, Chicago, IL: University of Chicago Press.

Freidson, E. (1970) *The Profession of Medicine: A Study of the Sociology of Applied Knowledge*, New York: Dodd Mead.

Frosh, P. (2001) "To Thine Own Self be True: The Discourse of Authenticity in Mass Cultural Production," *Communication Review*, vol. 4: 541–57.

Furnham, A. (1996) "In Search of Suckers," *Fortune*, October 14: 79–85.

Furusten, S. (1999) *Popular Management Books*, London: Routledge.

Gamson, J. (1994) *Claims to Fame: Celebrity in Contemporary America*, Berkeley, CA: University of California Press.

Gardner, W.L., Avolio, B.J., Luthans, F., May, D.R., and Walumbwa, F. (2005) "Can You See the Real Me? A Self-Based Model of Authentic Leader and Follower Development," *Leadership Quarterly*, vol. 16, no. 3: 343–72.

Gemmill, G. and Oakley, J. (1992) "Leadership: An Alienating Social Myth?", *Human Relations*, vol. 45, no. 2: 113–29.

George, B. (2003) *Authentic Leadership: Rediscovering the Secrets to Creating Lasting Value*, San Francisco, CA: Jossey-Bass.

Gibson, J.W. and Tesone, D.V. (2001) "Management Fads: Emergence, Evolution, and Implications for Managers," *Academy of Management Review*, vol. 15, no. 4: 122–33.

Gimein, M., Dash, E., Munoz, L., and Sung, J. (2002) "You Bought, They Sold," *Fortune*, 2 September: 64.

Gioia, D.A. and Thomas, J.B. (1996) "Image, Identity and Issue Interpretation: Sensemaking During Strategic Change in Academia," *Administrative Science Quarterly*, vol. 41: 370–403.

Gioia, D., Schultz, M., and Corley, K. (2000) "Organizational Identity, Image, and Adaptive Instability," *Academy of Management Review*, vol. 25, no. 1: 63–81.

Goldman, L., Burke, M., and Blakeley, K. (2007) "The Celebrity 100; Oprah, Tiger, Spielberg, Madonna and the Rest of the Biggest of the Big Shots," *Forbes*, 2 July: 82.

Goldman, R. and Papson, S. (1996) *Sign Wars: The Cluttered Landscape of Advertising*, New York: Guilford.

Greatbatch, D. and Clark, T. (2005) *Management Speak: Why We Listen to What Management Gurus Tell Us*, London: Routledge.

Greenleaf, R. (1977) *Servant Leadership: A Journey Into the Nature of Legitimate Power and Greatness*, New York: Paulist Press.

Grint, K. (2005) *Leadership: Limits and Possibilities*, London: Palgrave Macmillan.

Gross, D. (1996) *Forbes Greatest Business Stories of All Time*, New York: John Wiley.

Guthey, E. (1997) "Ted Turner's Media Legend and the Transformation of Corporate Liberalism," *Business and Economic History*, vol. 26, no. 1: 184–99.

Guthey, E. (2001) "Ted Turner's Corporate Crossdressing and the Shifting Image of American Business Leadership," *Enterprise and Society: The International Journal of Business History*, vol. 2, no. 1: 111–42.

Guthey, E. (2004) "New Economy Romanticism, Narratives of Corporate Personhood, and the Antimanagerial Impulse," in Lipartito, K. and Sicilia, D.S. (eds) *Crossing Corporate Boundaries: History, Politics, Culture*, New York: Oxford University Press: 321–42.

Guthey, E. and Jackson, B. (2003) "Open Season: Critical Perspectives on the Celebrity CEO Backlash," paper presented at the Academy of Management Meeting in Seattle, Washington.

Guthey, E. and Jackson, B. (2005) "CEO Portraits and the Authenticity Paradox", *Journal of Management Studies*, vol. 42, no. 5: 1057–82.

Guthey, E. and Jackson. B. (2008) "Revisualizing Image in Leadership and Organization Studies," in Barry, D. and Hansen, H. (eds), *Sage Handbook on New and Emerging Approaches to Management and Organization*, London: Sage: 84–92.

Guthey, E., Langer, R., and Morsing, M. (2006) "Corporate Social Responsibility Is a Management Fashion—So What?" in Morsing, M. and Beckmann, S. (eds), *Strategic CSR Communication*, Copenhagen: Djøf Publishers: 39–58.

Hall, S. (1981) "Notes on Deconstructing the Popular," in Samuel, R. (ed.) *People's History and Socialist Theory*, London: Routledge: 227–49.

Hammer, M. and Champy, R. (1993) *Reengineering the Corporation: A Manifesto for Business Revolution*, London: Nicholas Brealey.

Hammonds, K. (2002) "The Secret Life of the CEO: Do They Even Know Right from Wrong?", *Fast Company*, October: 81–9.

Handy, C. (2006) *The New Philanthropists*, London: Heinemann.

Hatch, M.J. and Schultz, M. (1997) "Relations Between Organisational Culture, Identity and Image," *European Journal of Marketing*, vol. 31, no. 5: 356–65.

Hayward, M.L.A., Rindova, V.P., and Pollock T.G. (2004) "Believing One's Own Press: The Causes and Consequences of CEO Celebrity", *Strategic Management Journal*, vol. 25, no. 7: 637–53.

Heenan, D.A. and Bennis, W.B. (1999) *Co-Leaders: The Power of Great Partnerships*, New York: John Wiley.

Heider, F. (1958). The Psychology of Interpersonal Relations, New York: Wiley.

Hirsch, P. (1972) "Processing Fads and Fashions: An Organization–Set Analysis of Cultural Industry Systems", *American Journal of Sociology*, vol. 77, no. 4: 639–59.

Huczynski, A. (2007) [1993] *Management Gurus*, revised edition, London: Routledge.

Huey, J. and Sookdeo, R. (1999) "The New Post-Heroic Leadership," *Fortune*, vol. 129: 42–50.

Iacocca, L. and Kleingfeld, S. (1988) *Talking Straight*, London: Sidgwick & Jackson.

Iacocca, L. and Novak, W. (1985) *IACOCCA: An Autobiography*, London: Sidgwick.

Ibarra, H. (1999) "Provisional Selves: Experimenting with Image and Identity in Professional Adaptation," *Administrative Science Quarterly*, vol. 44, no. 4: 764–92.

Isaacson, W. (1997) "In Search of the Real Bill Gates", *Time*, vol. 149, no. 2, January 13: 44ff.

Jackson, B. (2001) *Management Gurus and Management Fashions: A Dramatistic Inquiry*, London: Routledge.

Jackson, B. (2002) "A Fantasy Theme Analysis of Three Guru-Led Management Fashions," in Clark, T. and Fincham, R. (eds) *Critical Consulting: New Perspectives on the Management Advice Industry*, Oxford: Blackwell: 172–88.

Jackson, B. and Guthey, E. (2006) "Putting the Visual into the Social Construction of Leadership," in Shamir, B., Pillai, P., Bligh, M.C., and Uhl-Bien, M. (eds), *Follower-Centred Perspectives on Leadership: A Tribute to the Memory of James R. Meindl*, Greenwich, CT: Information Age Publishing, 167–86.

Jackson, B. and Parry, K. (2001) *The Hero Manager: Learning from New Zealand's Top Executives*, Auckland: Penguin.

Jones, C. and Thornton, P. (2005) "Introduction to Transformations in Cultural Industries," *Research in the Sociology of Organizations*, vol. 23: ix–xix.

Kaufman, W. (1968) *The Portable Nietzsche*, New York: Viking.

Kellaway, L. (2004) "So I Need to Be More Like Me? That's a Dreadful Idea," *Financial Times*, 8 March: 10.

Kellerman, B. (2008) *Followership: How Followers Are Creating Change and Changing Leaders*, Boston, MA: Harvard Business School Publishing.

Khurana, R. (2002a) *Searching for a Corporate Saviour: The Irrational Quest for Charismatic CEOs*, Princeton, NJ: Princeton University Press.

Khurana, R. (2002b) "The Curse of the Superstar CEO," *Harvard Business Review*, vol. 80, no. 9: 3–8.

Kieser, A. (1997) "Rhetoric and Myth in Management Fashion," *Organization*, vol. 4, no. 1: 49–74.

Krass, P. (1997) *The Book of Business Wisdom*, New York: John Wiley.

Krohe, J. (2004) "Look Who's Talking," *Across the Board*, vol. 41, no. 4: 1–7.

Lampel, J., Lant, T., and Shamsie, J. (eds) (2006) *The Business of Culture: Strategic Perspectives on Entertainment and Media*, London: Routledge.

Lash, S. (2007) "Power after Hegemony: Cultural Studies in Mutation?", *Theory, Culture, and Society*, vol. 24, no. 3: 55–78.

Leaf, C. (2002) "White-Collar Criminals. Enough is Enough. They Lie They Cheat They Steal and They've Been Getting Away with It for Too Long," *Fortune*, 18 March: 60–9.

Leonhardt, D. and Sorkin, A.S. (2002) "Reining in the Imperial CEO," *New York Times*, 15 September: 31.

Lewin, K. (1951) *Field Theory in Social Science*, New York: Harper.

Lewis, M. (2000) *The New New Thing: A Silicon Valley Story*, New York: W.W. Norton.

Liebovitz, A. (1983) *Photographs*, New York: Pantheon.

Lippmann, W. (1922) *Public Opinion*, New York: Macmillan.

Livingston, J. (1992) "How to Succeed in Business without Really Trying: Remarks on Martin Sklar's Corporate Reconstruction of American Capitalism," *Business and Economic History*, vol. 21: 30–5.

London, S. (2003) "Why Are the Fads Fading Away?", *Financial Times*, 12 June: 14.

Lowe, J. (2001) *Welch: An American Icon*, New York: John Wiley & Sons.

Lustig, R.J. (1982) *Corporate Liberalism: The Origins of Modern American Political Theory, 1890–1920*, Berkeley, CA: University of California Press.

Lutz, C. and Collins, J. (1993) *Reading National Geographic*, Chicago, IL: University of Chicago Press.

Manz, C. and Sims, H. (1991) "Superleadership: Beyond the Myth of Heroic Leadership," *Organizational Dynamic*, vol. 19, no. 4: 18–35.

Marchand, R. (1998) *Creating the Corporate Soul: The Rise of Public Relations and Corporate Imagery in American Big Business*, Berkeley, CA: University of California Press.

Marshall, P.D. (1997) *Celebrity and Power: Fame in Contemporary Culture*, Minneapolis, MN: University of Minnesota Press.

McCain Campaign (2008) "Celeb" (Political Advertisement), http://www.johnmccain.com last accessed September 29, 2008.

Meindl, J.R., Ehrlich, S.B., and Dukerich, J.M. (1985) "The Romance of Leadership", *Administrative Science Quarterly*, vol. 30, no. 1: 78–102.

Micklethwait, J. and Wooldridge, A. (1996) *The Witch Doctors*, London: Heinemann.

Mirzoeff, N. (1999) *An Introduction to Visual Culture*, London: Routledge.

Microsucks (2008a) A satirical website at http://www.microsucks.com, last accessed on July 28, 2008.

Microsucks (2008b) A satirical website at http://www.notagoth.com/microsucks/, last accessed on July 28, 2008.

Mitchell, W.J.T. (1995) *Picture Theory: Essays on Verbal and Visual Representation*, Chicago, IL: University of Chicago Press.

Mitchelson, W. and Calloway, M. (2006) "How to Avoid Letting a 'Perp Walk' Turn Into a Parade," *National Law Journal*, 21 March: S1.

Mizruchi, M. (2004) "Berle and Means Revisited: The Governance and Power of Large U.S. Corporations," *Theory and Society*, vol. 33, no. 5: 579–617.

Morgan, G. (1996) *Images of Organization*, London: Sage.

Morris, J.A., Brotheridge, C.M., and Urbanski, J.C. (2005) "Bringing Humility to Leadership: Antecedents and Consequences of Leader Humility," *Human Relations*, vol. 58, no. 10: 1323–50.

Mouly, S. and Sanakran, J. (2000) "The Tall Poppy Syndrome in New Zealand: An Exploratory Investigation," proceedings of the 2nd Conference of the International Association of Insight and Action, Brisbane.

Mulvey, L. (1975) "Visual Pleasure and Narrative Cinema," *Screen*, vol. 16, no. 3: 6–18.

Murray, M., Silverman, R.E., and Hymowitz, C. (2002) "Executive Affairs: GE's Jack Welch Meets His Match in Divorce Court—Stymied Early On, Ex-CEO Drops His Own Bombshell; Another Icon Tarnished?", *Wall Street Journal*, 27 November: A1.

Mydans, S. (2006) "Communist Vietnam Lunges for Capitalism's Brass Ring," *New York Times*, 27 April: 3.

Negus, K. (2002) "The Work of Cultural Intermediaries and the Enduring Distance between Production and Consumption," *Cultural Studies*, vol. 16, no. 4: 501–15.

Nocera, J. (2002) "System Failure: Corporate America Has Lost Its Way. Here's a Road Map for Restoring Confidence," *Fortune*, 24 June: 62ff.

O'Brien, T. (2005) *TrumpNation: The Art of Being the Donald*, New York: Business Plus.

O'Neal, M. (2002) "Coming Up Roses In a Downcast Year," *New York Times*, 29 December: 1.

O'Neill, W.J. (2004) *Sports Leaders and Success: 55 Top Sports Leaders and How They Achieve Greatness*, New York: McGraw-Hill.

O'Reilly, B. (2000) "The Power Merchant," *Fortune*, 17 April: 148–56.

Parker, I. (1989) *The Crisis in Modern Social Psychology, and How to End It*, London: Routledge.

Parker, M. (2006) "The Counter Culture of Organisation: Towards a Cultural Studies of Representations of Work," *Consumption, Markets and Culture*, vol. 9, no. 1: 1–15.

Pearce, S.L. and Conger, J.A. (eds) (2003) *Shared Leadership: Reframing the Hows and Whys of Leadership*, Thousand Oaks, CA: Sage Publications.

Peterson, R.A. (1979) "Revitalizing the Culture Concept," *Annual Review of Sociology*, vol. 5: 137–66.

Peterson, R. and Anand, N. (2004) "The Production of Culture Perspective," *Annual Review of Sociology*, vol. 30: 311–34.

Pfeffer, J. (1977) "The Ambiguity of Leadership," *Academy of Management Review*, vol. 2, no. 1: 104–12.

Pine, J. and Gilmore, J. (1999) *The Experience Economy*, Boston, MA: Harvard Business School Press.

Pollock, E.J. (1999) "New Management: Twilight of the Gods: The CEO as an Icon Hits a Down Cycle," *Wall Street Journal Europe*, 5 January: 1.

Raelin (2003) *Creating Leaderful Organisations: How to Bring out Leadership in Everyone*, San Francisco, CA: Berrett-Koehler.

Rein, I.J., Kotler, P., and Stoller, M.R. (1987) *High Visibility*, New York: Dodd, Mead & Company.

Rejai, M. and Phillips, K. (2004) "Leadership Theory and Human Nature," *Journal of Political and Military Sociology*, vol. 32, no. 2: 185–92.

Rindova, V.P., Pollock, T.G., and Hayward, M.L.A. (2006) "Celebrity Firms: The Social Construction of Market Popularity," *Academy of Management Review*, vol. 31, no. 1: 50–71.

Roddick, A. (1991) *Body and Soul*, London: Ebury Press, Random Century.

Rojek, C. (2001) *Celebrity*, Chicago: University of Chicago Press.

Rosenblum, B. (1978) "Style as Social Process," *American Sociological Review*, vol. 43, June: 422–38.

Ross, A. (ed.) (1988) *Universal Abandon? The Politics of Postmodernism*, Minneapolis, MN: University of Minnesota Press.

Røvik, K.A. (2002) "The Secrets of the Winners: Management Ideas that Flow," in Sahlin-Andersson, K. and Engwall, L. (eds) *The Expansion of Management Knowledge: Carriers, Flows and Sources*, Stanford, CA: Stanford University Press: 113–44.

Russo, F. (2007) "Leading! Without! Tom! Peters!", *Time*, 26 March: 6.

Samuels, D. (2008) "Shooting Britney," *Atlantic Monthly*, April: 15ff.

Sargant, W. (1997 [1957]) *The Battle for the Mind*, Cambridge: Malor.

Savedoff, B. (2000) *Transforming Images: How Photography Complicates the Picture*, Ithaca, NY: Cornell University Press.

Scheidel, T.M. (1967) *Persuasive Speaking*, Glenview, IL: Scott Foresman.

Schlender, B. et al. (2007) "Power 25," *Fortune*, 10 December: 116.

Schroeder, J.E. (2002) *Visual Consumption*, London: Routledge.

Seligman, M.E.P. and Csikszentmihalyi, M. (2000) "Positive Psychology," *American Psychologist*, vol. 55, no. 1: 5–14.

Semler, R. (1993) *Maverick*, London: Century.

Shamir, B., Pillai, P., Bligh, M.C., and Uhl-Bien, M. (eds) (2007) *Follower-Centred Perspectives on Leadership*, Greenwich, CN: IAP Publishing.

Shand, A. (2002) "Time We Got Uber the Mensch Thing," *Australian Financial Review*, 5 November: 9.

Sinclair, A. (2007) *Leadership for the Disillusioned: Moving Beyond Myths and Heroes to Leading that Liberates*, Crows Nest, Australia: Allen & Unwin.

Skapinker, M. (2003) "CEO: (n) Greedy Liar with Personality Disorder," *Financial Times*, 2 July: 8.

Sloan, A.P. (1963) *My Years with General Motors*, New York: Doubleday.

Sontag, S. (2004) "Regarding the Torture of Others," *New York Times Magazine*, 23 May.

Spell, C. (1999) "Where Do Management Fashions Come from, and How Long Do They Stay for?", *Journal of Management History*, vol. 5: 334–48.

Spell, C. (2001) "Management Fashions: Where Do They Come from, and Are They Old Wine in New Bottles?", *Journal of Management Inquiry*, vol. 10: 358–73.

Sroka, D. (2007) "Bill Gates Crossing the Delaware," http://www.gizmodo.com, last accessed on June 15, 2008. (Permission courtesy of Daniel Sroka, http://www.danielsroka.com.)

Staw, B.M. (1975) "Attribution of the Cause of Performance: A General Alternative Interpretation of Cross-Section Research on Organization," *Organizational Behavior and Human Performance*, vol. 13: 414–32.

Storey, J. (2004) "Changing Theories of Leadership and Leadership Development," in Storey, J. (ed.), *Leadership in Organizations: Current Issues and Key Trends*, London: Routledge: 11–37.

Strati, A. (1992) "Aesthetic Understanding of Organisational Life," *Academy of Management Review*, vol. 17, no. 3: 568–81.

Strati, A. and Guillet de Montoux, P. (2002) "Introduction: Organizing Aesthetics," *Human Relations*, vol. 55, no. 7: 755–66.

Suddaby, R. and Greenwood, R. (2001) "The Colonization of Knowledge: Product Commodification as a Dynamic of Change in Professional Service Firms," *Human Relations*, vol. 54, no. 7: 933–53.

Symonds, W. (2002) "Tyco: How Did They Miss a Scam so Big?", *BusinessWeek*, 20 September: 40.

Szymanski, J. (director), Henchy, C. (producer), and McKay, A. (writer) (2008) "Paris Does Politics, 1 and 2" (satiric video), http://www.funnyordie.com, last accessed on October 8, 2008.

Tagg, J. (1988) *The Burden of Representation: Essays on Photographies and Histories*, Minneapolis, MI: University of Minnesota Press.

Taylor, H. (1900) "The Trust Giant's Point of View: 'What a Funny Little Government,'" illustration in *Verdict Magazine*, 22 January.

ten Bos, R. and Heusinkveld, S. (2007) "The Gurus' Gusto: Management Fashion, Performance and Taste," *Journal of Organizational Change Management*, vol. 20, no. 3: 304–25.

The Economist (2002) "Leaders: Fallen Idols," 4 May: 11.

The Economist (2006) "The Birth of Philanthrocapitalism," 23 February: 9.

Thomas, C.B. (2007) "The Space Cowboys," *Time Magazine*, 5 March: 52.

Toronto Star (2002) "How Celebrity CEOs Failed to Deliver," 24 August: A1.

Tran, T. (2006) "Bill Gates Could Help Vietnam Technology," press release from the Associated Press, 24 April, http://www.bgnews.com, last accessed on June 15, 2008.

Treacy, M. and Wiersema, F. (1995) *The Discipline of Market Leaders: Choose Your Customers, Narrow Your Focus, Dominate Your Market*, Reading, MA: Addison Wesley.

Turner, G. (2004) *Understanding Celebrity*, London: Sage.

Turner, G., Bonner, F., and Marshall, P.D. (2000) *Fame Games: The Production of Celebrity in Australia*, Cambridge: New York: Cambridge University Press.

Useem, J. (2002) "Special Issue: The CEO under Fire: From Heroes to Goats . . . and Back Again?", *Fortune*, 18 November: 41.

Wade, J., Porac, J., Pollock, T., and Graffin, S. (2006) "The Burden of Celebrity: The Impact of CEO Certification Contests on CEO Pay and Performance," *Academy of Management Journal*, vol. 49, no. 4: 643–60.

Watson, T. J. (1994) "Management 'Flavours of the Month': Their Role in Managers' Lives", *International Journal of Human Resource Management*, vol. 5, no. 4: 893–909.

Watson, T.J. (2003) *Sociology, Work and Industry*, 4th edition, London: Routledge.

Weick, K. (1979) *The Social Psychology of Organizing*, Reading, MA: Addison Wesley.

Weidner, D. (2008) "Are More CEOs Headed for Unemployment?", httm://www.marketwatch.com, last accessed on June 10.

Wells, L. (1997) *Photography: A Critical Introduction*, London: Routledge.

Witzel, M. (2003) *Fifty Key Figures in Management*, London: Routledge.

Index

Printed in the United States
by Baker & Taylor Publisher Services